POWER

Their Uses and Abuses in Human Relations

Gerald Alper

POWER PLAYS

Their Uses and Abuses in Human Relations

Gerald Alper

International Scholars Publications
San Francisco - London - Bethesda
1998

Library of Congress Cataloging-in-Publication Data

Alper, Gerald.
    Power plays : their uses and abuses in human relations / Gerald
    Alper.
        p. cm.
    Includes bibliographical references and index.
    ISBN 1-57309-267-3 (hc : alk. paper). -- ISBN 1-57309-259-2 (pb :
    alk. paper)
    1. Control (Psychology) I. Title.
    BF632.5.A465   1998
    158.2--dc21   97-51293
                                                                      CIP

Editorial Inquiries:
International Scholars Publications
7831 Woodmont Avenue, #345
Bethesda, MD 20814

To order: (800) 55-PUBLISH

FOR SALLY LAMB

TABLE OF CONTENTS

PREFACE

Historically, the concept of power has been called upon to explain the casualties of human relating. Alfred Adler (1956) saw power operating as a maladaptive compensation of an underlying inferiority complex. Pioneer games theorists such as Eric Berne (1964) conceived of power plays as the unfortunate, although inevitable side effect of a reductionist state of mind which views interrelating as a series of either winning or losing behavioral strategies. Taking a different tack, double bind therapists such as Jay Haley (1963), cognitive therapists such as Albert Ellis and direct interventionists such as Milton Erickson have considered ways in which power, as a benign strategy of control, can be therapeutically harnessed. Biologists such as Richard Dawkins (1996) have depicted advantages in adaptive power as a driving force throughout evolution. While traditionally psychoanalysts have borrowed from Freud's (1915) discussion of mania as a collapse of the distinction between ego and super ego: his description of the so-called adult triumphs of the ego as unconscious derivatives of a glorious but bygone, buried period of infantile omnipotence; and a vigorous, exciting, anal, sadistic stage of mastery of somatic urges.

In light of this, there is a surprising lack of contemporary interest in and comment on the dynamics of power transactions as pertains to the individual. Significantly, in perhaps the most exhaustive modern dictionary of key psychoanalytic concepts--J. Laplanche and J.B. Pontalis' classic The Language of Psychoanalysis (1973)--power does not appear as even a single entry. By contrast, when it is discussed today, it is from an increasingly politicized standpoint: typically in terms of the authoritarian abuses of people in power vis-à-vis the rights of the have nots. (For an especially brilliant examination of how this is played out in the comparatively esoteric world of psychoanalysis, see Adam Phillips' Terrors and Experts (1996), for my own approach to the same subject, see The Dark Side of the Analytic Moon (Alper, 1996), and for a radical view of how family and social power can determine the diagnosis of schizophrenia, see R.D. Laing's Sanity, Madness and the Family, 1964.)

In my book I suggest this may be because power has ironically become such a widely accepted and unconscious staple of everyday life that in order to be taken seriously it needs to be raised to a fever pitch, presented as an authentic crisis affecting the lives of millions--in short, politicized. In opposition to this, the phenomena of power that are explored here are primarily intrapsychic and interpersonal. Although the political, cultural and social institutionalization of power to some extent must be implicated in individual power transactions, an attempt has been made to tease out the personal as much as possible.

Accordingly, a major theme throughout is that the power operations that are not politicized are as abusive, if not more so, than those that are if only because they often go unrecognized. As I define it, a power transaction arises when there is a covert attempt to impose rules on the behavior of the other, rules, moreover, which, regardless of how they are rationalized (e.g., typically, as being "for your own good") are patently meant to benefit only one person (the antithesis, one might say, to the rationale underlying the multitude of bylaws, customs, and mores comprising the social contract, which is that everyone supposedly shall be collectively better off).

That such opportunistic strategies of control are almost ubiquitously embraced in our present-day culture is perhaps less surprising if one considers, from a psychoanalytic and psychodynamic standpoint, that the very structuralization of the human psyche--the relations of the ego to its defenses, the defenses to the fears and anxieties that are its target, and the super ego to the ego--can be seen, to a certain extent, as frozen power operations, the relics and mirror of infantile/childhood familial transactions that to a significant degree were originally laid down through the use of force. If power is based on a presumed inequity of psychic forces, then every time we respond because we feel we are being constrained to, or every time we endeavor to effectively pressure the other into something he or she does not appear to want to do, we are operating along the lines of power. And while it could therefore be argued that the dynamics of power are at least partially imprinted in the psyche, it does not follow we are obliged to accept such transactions as a dominant mode of action and reaction.

For there is a whole other style of relating that does not feed off the opportunities conferred by a superiority of force, that instead only comes into being when the use of force does not loom as a necessary or eleventh hour reprieve, when the power that one has seems muted, in the background, or rather in the service of the deeper needs of a true self seeking, not conquest of the other, but mutuality, spontaneous interchange and enriching rapport. I am talking, of course, about the psychic possibilities engendered by the desire, readiness and capacity for intimate engagement.

It is a second major theme of this book, then, that intimacy, being an intrinsically complex state of mind difficult to achieve, occurs rarely in our present day culture. Perhaps because of its scarcity, the reports of its death have been greatly exaggerated, and it is because of their hopelessness over attaining intimacy on their own merits, that people today often desperately look outside of themselves for an authority to enforce and provide them with a kind of guarantee of decent treatment that does not involve and will not tolerate the slightest abuse of power. The irony, of course, is that while power can be used to oust power, it cannot be used to command, conjure up or inspire love: perhaps the hidden agenda of the political correctness movement and what it secretly yearns for. Paradoxically only the consolidation of realistic trust, which entails the relinquishing of any covert aims to politicize the behavior of the other can begin to do that.

So far as I know, my book may be the first phenomenological treatment of power transactions between people from a non-political, psychodynamic, intrapsychic and interpersonal framework. As such, the focus is always on the solitary person and the singular perspective as seen through the prism of psychoanalytic psychotherapy.

Although the various power transactions, operations, plays and maneuvers that are presented are based on incidents reported by former patients of mine, they seem to me to occur just as often to people who are not involved in therapy.

Whenever clinical vignettes are presented they are interspersed or supplemented with a running commentary. My hope is that their accumulated weight will make the theme of this book convincingly come to life.

CHAPTER ONE
Abuses
"YOU HAVE TO TAKE CHANCES IN THE STREET"

The only thing that relieved the drudgery of working in a restaurant for Todd, an aspiring New York actor, was his friendship with Dominick. A fellow waiter, Dominick had recently arrived or fled from a suburb in Chicago where, as he would explain it, "they were beginning to close in on me." He meant an investigator connected with the district attorney's office who had invited him to come in for some questioning concerning a highly suspicious string of successful automobile accident insurance claims, all registered under aliases, and all occurring within the improbable time frame of just two years. "When the noose tightens, that's when I split," Dominick had chortled.

And telling it in the session, Todd, plainly delighted, had laughed, too. Although, growing up on the Lower East Side he had seen up close his share of authentic frightening tough guys, he had never been befriended by one, never been privy to the inner workings, the peculiar, hard-boiled, predator's perspective of someone who views the world he lives in as his prey. What's more, Dominick was not just another tough guy, he was a first encounter with a personality type-- searching for the right word, Todd had settled on the designation, "sociopath", recollected from a freshman psychology textbook, that, previously, had existed for him primarily on TV. A person who, while capable of being amiable enough, even generous to those he deemed as consorts, could be seemingly heartless, unconscionably vicious to anyone considered to have seriously crossed the line of necessary respect: such transgressors being treated to a menu of sucker punches, choke holds, martial arts terror tactics and threats of unbelievable violence.

On at least one occasion, Todd had been a spectator, and silent if somewhat gullible collaborator, to Dominick's psychic barbarism. Feeling increasingly persecuted by someone to whom he had mistakenly loaned three hundred, who was all but refusing to pay it back, precipitating a growing rent crisis, Todd had sought out the counsel of his new friend. To his surprise, Dominick had leaped at the opportunity, not only almost instantly outlining a plan of action, but offering his services as a backup in case things went wrong. For according to his analysis, the man plainly had no intention of paying what he owed, was counting on either stalling or bullying Todd into submission, and therefore needed to be shaken up a little bit and taught a lesson. What Todd had to do was to get physical, implying that there would be a serious fight if the money was not promptly repaid. And if that didn't work, if the bluff was called and it seemed trouble was about to break out, then Dominick, who would be waiting in the wings, would intercede.

It seemed simple enough, relatively safe, yet something of an adventure for Todd, who had had his last fist fight over ten years ago when he was in junior high school and who in no way thought of himself as a tough guy, as he waited for his deadbeat erstwhile friend who finally came out of the dingy restaurant they once worked in together and headed for the darkened parking lot where he knew Dominick would be handily nearby. Nevertheless, he was far more scared than he had anticipated, as he stepped suddenly in front of the man (as Dominick had instructed), who now seemed considerably meaner and stronger looking than he had remembered.

"Look, you have to pay me the three hundred dollars right away. I'm about to be evicted."

"What did you say?"

"I said you have to pay."

"Or?"

"There'll be consequences."

"And if I don't, whatcha gonna do?"

It was at this moment--when Todd realized that not only had he miserably failed, in spite of his best efforts, to intimate his man, but he was about to be gratuitously humiliated--that he saw Dominick, who had been hiding in the shadows, furiously blindside his unsuspecting victim, clamping on his windpipe with one massive forearm, and using his free right hand to cup the back of his head and slam his face against the front windshield of a nearby parked car. Never had Todd seen such a display of unbridled brutality ("it was like something you'd see in the movies," he'd say later with skittish reverence) and for one terrifying moment he thought Dominick had decided it would be necessary, in order to teach him a lesson, to drive his face through the windshield. But, no, just when it seemed either the man's nose or the glass would break, Dominick abruptly let up, spun him around, grabbed him by the throat with both hands, lifted him to his toes and, staring murderously, delivered what he personally considered the mother of all threats:

"Look in my eyes. I know who you are and where you live. If you don't pay, immediately, by tomorrow morning, I'm going to find you and put you in a wheelchair. Understand?"

Stupefied with fear, perhaps thinking he was being set up for a hit, the man dumbly nodded his assent, weakly turned to go, was kicked viciously on the side of the kneecap and, half limping, half running, desperately fled from the parking lot. But he had apparently learned his lesson, for upon arising the next morning, Todd discovered, lying on his kitchen floor, an envelope containing three hundred dollars that had been pushed under his front door by his former friend who, he would subsequently learn, had both quit his job and checked out of his apartment.

As genuinely appreciative as Todd was for the gangbusters backup, he could not refrain from mildly chastising Dominick for choosing to resort to violence without consulting beforehand with him. "Well, I could see you weren't getting anywhere with the guy," came the laconic retort. "But what if a cop had happened to come by?" persisted Todd, increasingly aware of an uncomfortable feeling that he had gotten in over his head. "You have to take chances in the street," replied Dominick, beginning to warm to his self-appointed role as Todd's mentor in mayhem. And when Todd, now more in awe than remonstrance, had questioned the point of threatening to put in a wheelchair someone he had never met before and who had never done anything to him, Dominick had triumphantly pounced on it as an opportunity to encapsulate his modus operandi: "I'm a master intimidator. If you make someone think that you're willing to seriously cripple them, they get awfully scared."

As Todd himself was aware, the acute self-consciousness of his own powerlessness that had brought him to therapy--his daily life as a non-working New York actor which consisted of being too depressed to submit to the ordeal of auditions, feeling demeaned by having to function as a professional food-bearer to strangers, while being steadily harassed by a manager who wanted him to be more energetic and enthusiastic about his work, and generally regarded by family and acquaintances as an entertaining, somewhat talented, but hopelessly unrealistic marginal character earmarked for failure--also made him susceptible to what he perceived as the sociopathic charisma of his new friend. Not surprisingly, in the months that followed, Dominick moved from being a narrative, thematic element to a presence in Todd's therapy.

His interest kindled by the bizarre encounter in the parking lot, Todd allowed himself for the first time, with the help of Dominick, to be indoctrinated in the code of the street: where power rules, where relating tends to be territorial rather than personal, where one makes one's way and earns one's reputation by demonstrating a capacity and readiness to defend one's rights, and where doing what is necessary to survive on a kind of inner city frontier, and not the attaintment of security, is the order of the day. The values of the street, as Todd would learn, in addition to charisma, were aggression, courage, a willingness to take big chances, rebelliousness, independence, tempered by fierce loyalty to one's neighborhood and friends (e.g., "never rat on your friend") where fidelity to the mores of the gang took precedence over everything else. And in this sense, the code of the street could be seen as a residue and primitivistic revamping of the turmoil of adolescence: the desperate need for peer approval transformed into the macho concern for one's "rep" and the hunger to be popular and included being fed by membership into a gang.

Because of its state of intrinsic dangerous contingency, surviving meant knowing not only how to fight, but "who not to mess with"--crack dealers, sworn-in members of violent gangs (typically sporting tattooed insignias) and hard core ex-cons who are likely to be carrying or have access to lethal weapons. The code of the street, therefore, depended on grasping a pecking order primarily based on brutal, sociopathic power--coolness in the face of extreme danger, ruthless opportunism, physical aggressiveness--one that scorned the traditional emblems of business, professional and financial prestige in mainstream American society. (For a marvelous analysis of what risks are considered worth taking and how they are calculated in the ordinary, non-sociopathic world, see Erving Goffman's classic essay, "Where The Action Is" (1967)). Finally, from a psychodynamic standpoint, the code of the street could be compared with the violent ethos of professional contact sports where similar values prevail: gang loyalty and neighborhood territorialism being analogous to the intense comraderie among fellow players, the ferocious competition with rival teams, and the commitment to risking life and limb in defense of one's turf (it is hardly surprising, therefore, that the heroes of the street come predominantly from the sports arenas).

As his therapist I was able to see that part of Todd's fascination with Dominick's frankly aberrant lifestyle was a reflection of a more pervasive absorption with certain cultural sociopathic elements. In addition to the obvious obsessive portrayal and celebration of violence in movies, in the videos and recordings of rap artists, in television's devotion to action-adventure thrillers, sensationalistic soap operas and the crunch time of big time professional sports, in the gory excesses of tabloid journalism, the increasingly mean-spirited putdowns of talk radio's shock jocks (the idea of asserting yourself through creatively, entertainingly and destructively tearing someone else apart), there was in the media and especially advertising, the presentation of ordinary life as the recommended pursuit of a series of pleasurable, but safe highs (e.g., the covert hedonistic philosophy expressed in "this is as good as it gets").

Reinforcing this was the addictive reliance on the attainment of emotional satisfaction through an assortment of high-tech quick fixes: the belief that human conflict and discontent were by-products of a dysfunctional biochemistry that were best repaired by mood-altering and deficiency-replenishing drugs; the escalating use and allure, as well, of toxic, illicit substances, and the seemingly insatiable hunger for ever faster-acting, positive-thinking cures for any and all of life's ills, all of which engendered a widespread and growing cynicism that viewed transactions between people as being either money-driven or based on the politics of power; and that regarded traditional morality as perhaps idealistically reassuring although contemporarily irrelevant, embracing instead a brand of pop existentialism that favored creating your own ad hoc systems of values as you went along. Such a view took solace in the building of the information highway and spread of the Internet and often found the computer model of the human brain, with its implicit message that people are ultimately reducible to machines, to be an unconscious validation of their impersonal, anonymous style of relating and their nihilistic belief that people and relationships are interchangeable units. And, lastly, there was undeniable perverse satisfaction in the blatant hollowness of the criminal justice system (as revealed in the course of the televised proceedings of the O.J. Simpson trial) which seems to depend on who can muster the more telling and expedient gamesmanship which in turn often comes down to who can be more opportunistically vicious.

In particular, there seemed to be one element that served as a ready transitional link between mainstream culture and the sociopathic code of the street: the art of being cool. Partly because it is so routinely glorified by the media and in advertising (e.g., Joe Camel being just one notorious example among many), it is overlooked how some of the defining qualities of this much admired contemporary state of mind--remaining strikingly, narcissistically uninvolved and tantalizingly non-responsive regardless of the emotional context, seemingly always slickly in control of one's deeper feelings, with an ability to get over and maneuver oneself out of the tightest spots--coincide with frank sociopathic behavior. It is therefore cool to be able to pull off a power coup in any sphere of one's life. Getting a lot for a little, placing a smart bet or simply being incredibly lucky (e.g., winning the lottery) are considered cool. One way to understand the meaning of being cool is to look at what is not cool. To be in a situation in which one does not have the upper hand, to become overly emotional, to allow oneself to feel discouraged, deprived, depressed, to pursue someone who is not interested in you, to wind up in therapy, to fail, to act unconfidently, to be tender and nurturing in an intimate way--are not cool.

By contrast, the containment rather than the investment of emotions (the sociopathic version of this would be the capacity to keep one's head, in the fashion of Dominick, in a violent emotional storm) is the hallmark of being cool, and the appellation is rarely applied to someone who is passionately committed to what they are doing, as opposed to just doing their own thing (see Christopher Bollas, 1995, for a profound discussion of the differences between obsessional and passionate involvement).

It was this quality of sociopathic cool, however, that seemed to Todd beyond his comprehension or that he could not accept, yet most intrigued him. For while he could find vicarious release in the visceral excitement entailed in Dominick's occasional gonzo acts of intimidation, and could rationalize them as being weirdly entertaining instances of nutty macho behavior, he could not understand the ice water-in-the veins composure of someone who, without a sign of trepidation, could plot and execute what he fondly referred to as scams or a con game (although he suspected that he had been targeted by a police computer as a result of his Chicago escapades as someone who was likely to assume aliases, rig phony automobile accident claims and try to collect from gullible insurance companies, Dominick did not otherwise feel restrained when it came to dipping into his considerable repertoire of con games).

When I asked Todd what he, or what Dominick meant by scams and con games, he was eager to share with me his recently acquired inside information. A scam, to be distinguished from a con game, was a devious scheme designed to extract money anonymously, without being detected, whether from an individual or a company. Trying to collect on a fraudulent insurance claim was a scam. Procuring a substantial sum of travelers' checks, reporting them stolen and then being reimbursed by the company who issued the travelers' checks, while almost simultaneously having a cohort cash the alleged stolen checks, thereby doubling your money, was a scam. Having access to, or stealing a private blank check from a wealthy individual for whom, say, one has worked, arranging for an ally whose handwriting would be unknown and untraceable to fill in a hefty amount, forge the owner's name, and the promptly cash it in a check-cashing place, is a scam.

By contrast, a con or confidence game is an interpersonal scheme in which one person, the con man, pretends to give his confidence to another, the mark, for the purpose of gaining his trust in order to subsequently swindle him. In a typical con game, the mark is led to believe he is being invited to share in the spectacular profits of a unique but sure-fire financial venture. In exchange, all the mark has to do is provide some needed assistance in the form of some short term, comparatively nominal cash, to be repaid almost immediately. Once the mark--seduced by spurious flattery and tantalized by the prospect of his greediest fantasies on the verge of being realized--hands over his money, the transaction is complete and the confidence man, if he can help it, is never seen or heard from again.

Whetting my own interest as Todd narrated his growing fascination with the mechanics of scams and con games were personal memories (not uncommon, I think, to veteran New Yorkers such as myself) of encounters with individuals (panhandlers, typically) who, admittedly on a minor, amateurish scale, had tried to con me. There was, for example, the time I heard the buzzer ring in my office indicating someone in the street wanted to be admitted into the building and then-- when I had not responded because the person had failed to identify himself over the intercom--seemed to hear the buzzer continue to ring in some adjacent apartments. Five minutes later I had almost completely put this out of my mind, when the bell to my fourth floor office unexpectedly rang. I opened the door upon a thin, sallow-cheeked man who was breathing heavily and who plainly appeared to be under the weather:

"I'm your first floor neighbor. Look, I'm really sick, my roommate has gone out and I need to borrow some money for a cab to go to the hospital. I'll pay you back as soon as my roommate comes back. Please."

Odd as this sounded, I was taken in by the man's quavering voice and forlorn demeanor and was seriously pondering whether to extend a five or ten dollar loan to a complete stranger when, with a jolt, I remembered and connected the buzzer I had recently heard ringing in a number of apartments. All at once I realized that it had been this man standing in my doorway who had come from the street and began randomly buzzing apartments in the hope of being admitted, who obviously did not live in the building (now it dawned on me how improbable it was that not once had I ever seen my alleged first floor neighbor) and who, sick or not, had no intention to taking a taxi to the hospital but was endeavoring to obtain money for entirely different purposes, money which he certainly did not intend to pay back.

Fortified by my insight, I respectfully, and regretfully (for how could I be sure my inferences were at all valid?) declined his request for emergency cab fare (a refusal I was relieved that he graciously--or manipulatively, to play upon my manifest guilt--accepted: "I understand"). Ten minutes later, when I had to leave the office, my suspicions were patently confirmed--I noticed the same man on the stoop of another building about a block away randomly pressing one buzzer after another.

Ironically, this incident was not unlike another which had occurred twenty years previously, shortly after I had moved into Manhattan. A man with a deflated tire slung around his shoulder and carrying a large tin can had accosted me in the street: he had run out of gas and needed to get back to his home in New Jersey but discovered he had somehow forgotten his wallet. Assuring me that if I furnished him with my name and address he would pay me back as soon as he arrived home, he asked if I could help him out with a much needed loan. For a moment the authenticity and naturalism of the tire hanging from his shoulder, the tin can, and the oddness of his tale of traveler's distress which had never before been presented to me in such fashion, led me to wonder if he might be telling the truth. But reason quickly prevailed. It did not make sense that someone would seemingly earnestly entrust himself to a complete stranger to bail him out of an emergency situation as opposed to soliciting the assistance of a trained policeman. The more I thought about it, the more I studied the man before me whose appearance was beginning to strike me as closer to that of a vagrant than to the car and home owner he proclaimed himself to be, the more I realized how much I disliked being played for a mark. And so resolved, I indicated politely that I could not help him.

In the years that followed I was accosted in the same way, with only the slightest of variations, perhaps a dozen times and became reluctantly wise in the ways of duplicitous panhandlers. But I had never before been afforded a glimpse into the state of mind of a real confidence man and, as a psychotherapist, I was intrigued by the dynamics of the con games that were being depicted for me by Todd.

Over time, and from the standpoint of object relations, it appeared to me there was a structure to the con game. On the one hand, there was the con man, someone in possession of a secret power, a weapon that can powerfully but imperceptibly control the other. On this simple level, then, the con game works because you are in the know and they are the sucker. The skill that is obviously required to carry off the transaction without being apprehended and that can only be acquired through hard work is used to justify the profit that is dishonestly gained. Contrariwise, the characteristic lack of self-respect and gullibility of the mark are used to justify the exploitation to which they are subjected. (In the sociopath, perhaps through projective identification, the sense of a weak or powerless self which we all have, is put into the sucker and there safely despised and heartily punished).

Psychodynamically then the con game shows the all or nothing, either/or dichotomy typical of an obsessive desire for power. The perpetrator has divided up the interpersonal domain into a con artist who presumably knows all there is to know and a sucker who is to be carefully kept completely in the dark until it is too late. The enactment of a con game sponsors a transaction that is irrevocably destructive of any hope of mutuality: creating the hardest of zero sum games in which there can only be one winner and one loser and where what is lost is the self esteem that comes from a belief one can protect oneself--the victim awakening, instead, to a sense of betrayal and lingering violation.

From an interpersonal standpoint therefore, a con game can be viewed as an unconscious attempt to lure an unsuspecting other into a covert sadomasochistic contract in which there is to be a seduction--the establishment of a cozy comraderie in which a dream is shared of getting something of great value together--followed by a betrayal. For the confidence man who consciously conceives of relating as a series of strategic moves that result in a stunning payoff--unlike the typical denouément of one of Eric Berne's transactional games, 1960, the payoff here is a shocking theft of the other's peace of mind, akin to what Christopher Bollas has described in a different context in his great essay, "Violent Innocence", 1993--it may be that the unconscious pleasure of transient if illusory closeness with someone else followed by their profound irreparable disappointment in you, is as important an incentive as the money about to be swindled. It follows the con game can be used as a substitutive perverted technique for relating (in the sense of Khan, 1979).

This all or nothing dichotomy of the con game can be viewed as an example of psychical splitting: all knowledge, gratifying good feelings and prospects for pleasure are placed on one side and all disappointing illusion, deprivation and pain on the other. From an object relations framework, therefore, enacting a con game may be a way of splitting a relationship (analogous to the intrapsychic splitting of an object) as a defense against the possibility of mutuality. Indeed, splitting as an inability to integrate the good and bad aspects of an object, can be seen within the context of a relationship as the antithesis of mutuality.

Finally, a con game can represent an unconscious strategy for having an exciting, often passionate connection knowing that it will soon deconstruct with a violent bang. By traumatically abandoning the person, the confidence man insures that the violated mark will never forget him. Analogous to the physically abusive individual who secretly desires a bond with another without having to relate, he uses the con game as a magical vehicle for a lasting connection that can be forged with amazing rapidity--the sociopath relates through being the agent of trauma in the other and his perverted psychic legacy is to leave in his wake an abiding traumatic object relation.

THE LION'S SHARE

Because the sociopath is typically unaffected by the normative restraints of conscience, morality and social prohibitions, his pursuit, if not lust for power is easy to show. But what are the benefits of power and its relationship to the ordinary person, whether in or out of therapy, who is the proper subject of this book?

To begin with the obvious: it feels good to be in touch with what one believes is one's personal power, part of which is the sense of not being hurried; of having instead arrived at a secure inner space and of possessing an abundance of the resources needed to survive. It is a characteristic of the empowered person, therefore, that he moves at his own pace and sets his own agenda as though time waits on him and not vice versa. Not only can such an individual be careless, make mistakes and get away with it, but he can afford to allow others, if he wishes, to make mistakes and get away with it, too. Because having power means survival is not an issue, it can be liberating. Energy that would normally go into defensive measures can be used for exploratory and adventuresome interests. As a consequence, more options are made available. Spontaneity becomes possible, and there is room as well as psychic resources to invest in developing and expressing the self.

For all of these reasons, power can connote that one has established one's rightful psychic territory, is not being intruded upon and that interpersonal territorialism is not at stake. On the contrary, the feeling often is of psychological spaciousness, of inner riches, of satiety. One's primary needs have and will be met. The aura surrounding the person of power is therefore usually one of calm, the intrapsychic and interpersonal message seeming to be, "I have nothing to be desperate about." Because of this, one of the most common ways of demonstrating one's power is by exaggerating the difference between your state of relaxation and the other's comparative uneasiness. Analogous to the aggressive individual who strives to appear as though coming out ahead by never seeming to be on an equal affective or cognitive wavelength, someone wishing to demonstrate their power will make a point of seeming conspicuously less fraught than the other.

While the ordinary person, feeling empowered, may secretly enjoy the prospect, or fantasy, of receiving the lion's share of the benefits of whatever he is involved in, it is the sociopath like Dominick who will ruthlessly try to act this out. When the everyday need to occasionally display an advantageous power differential is translated into the code of the street, it manifests itself therefore often as the intent to intimidate.

Sociopathic intimidation, as practiced by someone like Dominick, combining the reflexive violence of the natural predator with a pathological absence of empathy for the victim's pain, is especially frightening. When the characteristic serenity of the empowered person is used to intimate the other, then the message insidiously changes from, "I have nothing to be desperate about" to "Nothing you can possibly do can make me desperate." Hollywood films celebrating the gangster lifestyle for purposes of vicarious titillation readily portray and carry to grotesque extremes such violent narcissistic indifference: in Prizzi's Honor, the protagonist hit man matter-of-factly notifies a banker who has witnessed a double murder that should he ever think

10

of informing on him, "There's no place on earth we can't get to"; in <u>Midnight Run,</u> the mafioso drug czar who has at last tracked down and come face to face with the former accountant who has stolen money from him, chillingly tells him, "You're going to die, then I'm going to go home, have a hot meal, find your wife and kill her."

It is terrifying to be on the receiving end of such sociopathic or criminal acts of intimidation because the message plainly is that no amount of conventional, social, legal or psychological pressure will deter them. And the exercise of power that cannot or will not be restrained, for which obstacles do not exist in its march to gratify itself, seems devouring. It is terrifying because it renders impotent the normally reliable evocative power of empathy which we count upon, among other things, to internally regulate the desire of the other to seriously harm us. By instead treating our true self as only an insignificant obstacle it actualizes a virtual world of evil possibilities from which, previously, we unconsciously felt protected. The sociopathic intimidator, by remaining empathically deaf and dumb to our naturally resonating humanity, is thereby enabled to use us as a thing. And once one is refused proper existential status--since our primary claim upon the other is that one is a human being entitled to the rights deriving from being the vessel of undeniable special sensibilities--anything is possible. To be sociopathically denied such indispensable existential recognition is therefore unconsciously equated with being stripped of one's birthright, tantamount to being suddenly and inexplicably told or treated as though you were not born of human parents.

It follows that a crucial difference between the ordinary person and the sociopath will be the manner in which they display power, especially their power, real and imagined, over the other. Although the ordinary person, in contrast to the sociopath, will obviously be more sensitive to the feedback of the other, he will typically try to show his power by imposing limits on their respective interpersonal fields of action. In other words, he will endeavor to be the one who sets or reinforces the boundaries on what can and cannot be done. The most common evidence that this is the case in our contemporary society is the ability to act unilaterally on you in ways that will have undeniable consequences and the classic American example is the company boss who can hire you, tell you exactly what to do and what not to do, and, when necessary, fire you. And the basic reaction of the recipient is the realization that "they have the power", the frustrated perception that there is an insurmountable disparity in the comparative ability of each party to behave in an autonomous, decisive manner. It is characteristic of such power that it appears immovable, wants to be admired rather than understood, respected, feared, complied with rather than interacted with, and makes a point of spurning feedback and reciprocity. <u>It unconsciously strives not to reveal a self, or itself, or express anything other than its strength, its force, its potential for an appreciable impact, harm, or unilateral change.</u>

YOU CAN'T FIGHT CITY HALL

An incident recounted to me by a patient perhaps can illustrate how it feels to experience yourself in the grip of impersonal power. Dennis was a disgruntled, thirty-five year old accountant who felt he had immersed himself monastically for ten years in a world of professional duties, but had remarkably little to show for it. He considered himself underpaid, unappreciated and in general discounted to an alarming degree. His love life offered few consolations: although unrelenting in his pursuit of the right woman--someone who would be deeply understanding, compassionate and willing to share a life with him--he was forever winding up with women who, as he would later ruefully conclude, had only wanted to use him in one way or another. Not surprisingly, he was hypersensitive to perceived slights, often ruminating aloud in sessions over telephone calls that were not returned, the failure of one person to say hello, the refusal of another to smile at him and, especially, the attempt by anyone to take advantage of him.

With this context in mind, Dennis had caught my attention when, visibly perturbed, he had announced that on the previous evening he had suffered the single greatest public humiliation of his life. What made it particularly galling was that the architect of his shame had been in his view the lowliest of public servants--a token booth clerk in the Manhattan subway transit system. This particular clerk, a heavyset, thirtyish, moon-faced woman, moreover had already incurred Dennis' ire on several previous occasions by plainly and rudely grimacing when he had presented her with coins instead of dollar bills in order to purchase some tokens (presumably because she had to take a little extra time to count them). He was therefore not happy when--sweating profusely in the record summer humidity he had simultaneously realized he had forgotten his wallet while managing to bring a token that did not seem to be working--he had been forced to solicit the aid of the erstwhile scowling booth clerk. Hoping the token and the obviousness of his predicament would do most of his talking for him, Dennis held it up about a foot from her eyes. "I tried the slots of four different turnstiles and it doesn't fit in any of them," he said flatly. Appraising the exhibited token in an instant and regarding her solicitor with a look of quizzical boredom, as though she had just been told something she had already heard hundreds of times before and had no need to hear again, she shot back, "It's the wrong token."

Feeling increasingly at her mercy, Dennis tried to act cool: "Could you please exchange it for me then?"

"I can't. You have to go to 31st Street and Eighth Avenue."

"But that's a mile away."

"You can't walk a mile?"

The tone of voice, pointedly saccharine and mimicking, had succeeded in not only infuriating Dennis, but had made him vow to himself that at whatever cost he would gain admittance into the subway station.

"No, I can't. Look, take this token and let me through the service entrance."

"I'll take the token, but I won't let you through."

"Yes, you can. Now take the token. I'll redeem it tomorrow, if you like. But let me through."

"Do you want me to lose my job?"

"Please, let me through."

"Don't you have a dollar fifty for a token?"

"I don't."

"You don't have a dollar fifty?" The same mocking, saccharine tone.

Aware there was no hope of prevailing unless he mastered his rage, Dennis tried to be politic. "Why don't you just trust me? I've been riding this subway daily for the past seven months."

"I've never seen you before in my life."

Desperate to make a connection, Dennis had what he considered a bright idea. "Do you remember the man last week who gave you a lot of nickels and dimes for some subway tokens?"

As though she had just heard a good one, the woman, moving her head derisively from side to side, chortled, "That was you?"

"Yes."

"You give me lots of change to count and you expect me to let you through for it?" (continuing to chortle).

Beginning to feel paranoid about the rush hour line that was queuing up at his back and--embarrassed by the voice of a tough guy growling at him to move on-- Dennis made one last try:

"Look, I've seen hundreds of young punks jump the turnstile and not pay their fare and nobody ever stops them. This may be the wrong token, but at least I paid for it."

As though he had finally uttered an undeniably sound point the woman slowly and judiciously nodded her head. "That's true. All right. You can go through, too."

Immensely relieved, believing he was about to be admitted, Dennis walked to the service door, grasped it and patiently waited for the releasing buzzer. When none was forthcoming, he moved over to a nearby turnstile and gingerly pressed his waist against the restraining metallic bar, half-hoping that either he would discover a way to ease through or that the clerk, true to her word, would somehow press a button that would mechanically move the turnstile. But once again nothing happened and looking back he saw the woman now preoccupied with making change and distributing tokens to a growing line of customers. It then dawned on Dennis that when she had told him he could go through, too, what she meant was, if he chose, he could act in the manner of a young punk and scale the turnstile bars without paying his fare. And so, thoroughly exasperated, that is what Dennis--hardly nimble at the age of thirty-five and never athletic to begin with--tried to do. Not surprisingly, he failed miserably: crashing his right shin into the bar of the turnstile as he attempted to swing his legs over the top, and falling backwards, hard, to the ground. Scrambling to his feet, to nip in the bud a rising sense of public shame, Dennis noted for the first time about ten customers, waiting in line to buy their tokens, intently studying him. Did they think he was trying to get in for free? Didn't they understand he had been given permission to go through by the token booth clerk?

Apparently not. A woman about fifty years of age, with white hair, but lean and mean looking, took a step towards him and with all the might in her lungs bellowed, "You're a grown man. Why don't you pay your fare?"

Feeling completely beaten, Dennis pathetically lofted his outdated token, was about to explicate and rectify the utterly misleading impression he was giving, thought better of it, dusted himself off, and miserably began walking the required mile to 31st Street and Eighth Avenue in order to exchange it.

Although extreme in form, this kind of an exchange, to a greater or lesser degree, probably occurs millions of times daily in our country. From an interpersonal standpoint, what is so striking about the interaction is its insistent, unrelenting negativity. Right from the beginning, if an opportunity for positive rapport is presented, it is instantly squelched: when Dennis approaches the booth clerk, holding his defunct token aloft, plainly a commuter in distress, he is pounced on for his ineptitude ("It's the wrong token"); when he offers to give her back the old token and asks to be let through now and to trust him to redeem the token tomorrow, she answers with exaggerated cynicism ("Do you want me to lose my job?"); and when he tries to portray himself as more than a random anonymous traveler, as, in fact, someone who has been regularly frequenting this particular subway station for the past seven months, she icily comments, "I've never seen you before in my life."

In every instance, there is a subversive, covert and willful strategy designed to create distance, so that the interaction as a whole could be fairly characterized as a flight from intimacy. This is hardly surprising in a functional relationship such as that between a token booth clerk and a commuter that is entirely based on role performance and the maintenance of power and therefore easily threatened by someone like Dennis who--far from being interested in who's in charge--wants a person who can relate to, empathize with and show special consideration for the unusual circumstances in which he finds himself. In other words, when the authority of the role player is treated as though irrelevant and what is sought is the capacity to interrelate, then the individual can become confused and annoyed as to why the other does not seem to accept, as the majority of people do, that the transaction can be conducted smoothly along purely formal, impersonal lines. In that case the atypical wish for understanding and rapport may be interpreted as only a lack of respect for their power and the desire to relate be seen--not as the expression of a legitimate need--but as a sign of contemptuous familiarity.

It follows the person in charge is then likely to defend herself by brandishing her most potent weapon--the capacity to exercise her power at the expense of the other in a decisively negative fashion (e.g., "I'll take the token, but I won't let you through"). Which, of course, in turn fosters resistance that often results in a fight, the fight initially being over whether power or intimacy is to be the appropriate basis for conducting the transaction and resolving the dispute. A favorite tactic then of the one with authority is to trash the character of the other: e.g., the token booth clerk mocking Dennis for not having a dollar and fifty cents on him, the implication being that at bottom this is only the protest of an indigent man. The hope now is that through shaming, it becomes almost impossible for the humiliated person to stand behind his claim that there is a valid need to relate. All the other can reasonably do instead is to angrily defend the credibility of the original actions in question, but by so doing, he has insidiously been driven into a power game--that of aggressive, and usually manipulative, counter-arguing. And it is obvious, when two people are upset with one another, that the person with power will win, if only because the consequences of her being angry are considerably greater than the consequences of the other being angry. The sword of Damocles, then, is that anytime she wishes to act out her animosity in a punitive way, she can simply use her power to frustrate whatever it seems the other most wants. Not surprisingly, when this is the case, anger tends to get expressed almost exclusively on her terms.

When there is antagonism between two people, it will be to the advantage of the person with the upper hand to pursue a transaction that is based on power rather than intimacy. This is because:

1.	Relating can be replaced by procedural steps.

2.	Conflicts between people can be externalized and referred to a preferred method of problem solving.

3.	The expression of a complex personal need can be translated into a request for necessary information and dealt with by instruction. The expression of clear frustration can be regarded as the outcome of an underlying ignorance or lack of sufficient technical and professional tools with which to gratify oneself, and the raising of self esteem issues, the desire to facilitate intimacy between factious parties, can be reduced to a communicational snafu.

4.	The manifestation of interpersonal discontent thereby tends to be denied. Instead of someone being obsessive, dismissive or arrogant, there is only a person who is behaving unprofessionally or incompetently (and if anyone does not accept this, there is something wrong with them).

5.	Finally, from this perspective, right and wrong, success and failure become and criteria for judging interactions between people. Another way to say this is that the inner psychic time of interrelating, which is not linear, has been converted to outer, instrumental time. When the dispensing of information or the enactment of stipulated procedures are thereby used to define the interpersonal transaction, then the time to relate is automatically annulled (and this, of course, means that a transaction based on power, by being able to control the onset and termination of the time needed for intimacy to develop--can thereby drastically curtail the ability or desire to relate).

One may ask why in a power struggle between unequal parties, it is necessary--as so often seems the case--to repeatedly reject the weaker party? Dennis, for example, after narrating his public humiliation, was quick to point out that right from the start (as soon as she had snapped, "It's the wrong token") he realized that this woman was going to resist and belittle him every inch of the way, but for some reason felt compelled to do whatever he could to persuade her to change her mind. Furthermore, he was aware that he became hooked on the token booth clerk's stubborn dismissal of him and found it secretly thrilling to go toe to toe with her, ready even to hop the turnstile and run the risk of being apprehended by an unsympathetic transmit plainclothesman. Rejection, it seemed, in spite of being demoralizing, could also be quite seductive.

It is almost as though the one who is in a position, or empowered to be the rejecter has thereby cast a spell of unavailability and the other, bewitched, does not desire the object so much as the object's approval. Attachment to a rejecting object then becomes an obsessive attempt to undo a toxic criticism that because it is so general, appears devastating, and the recipient understandably finds it is difficult to go on living or rest easy unless it is repealed. Reinforcing the unconscious hope that only a misunderstanding or temporary bad mood has been responsible for what has happened is denial that the rejection could possibly be serious, substantive and reflective of a characterological dissatisfaction with the person one takes oneself to be. After all, rejection represents nearly every person's worst nightmare: tantamount to having your most despicable qualities made public, passed judgment on and perpetuated in the consciousness of others. Devotion to a rejecting object, therefore, paradoxical as this may be, has two common sense strategies: persuade the rejector to change her opinion in a more favorable direction; or, by ingratiating oneself, to induce her to soften the harsh edges of disrespect and adopt a posture of at least pseudo civility. One of the most painful aspects of the rejection is the feeling of abandonment and betrayal that it almost immediately engenders. Even more painful than the pain of the specific content of the rejection is the pain that the other seemingly could not care less and feels entitled to not only withdraw all narcissistic supplies, possibilities of comfort, and nurturance but to willfully confine the person to a prison of contempt and, subsequently, desert them. In other words, what hurts is not so much their criticism--they can live with having terrible flaws provided they believe the other still has a basic respect and liking for them--but their hateful punishment. It is rejection's lethal combination of hate, punishment and complete lack of respect that is unbearable. Analogous to being accused of a serious crime one did not commit, it is something that cannot go unanswered. If a person does not stand up for themselves, in that case, then anyone can do anything to them and, to continue the analogy, being rejected can feel like being <u>accused, sentenced and punished by the other's superego for a crime one did not commit</u>. Since the accused cannot come out and say that for fear of renewal of the rejection, and since one now totally mistrusts the fairness, decency and objectivity of the accuser, one begins--akin to a criminal defense attorney--to use every manipulative, coercive or ingratiating trick in one's book to undermine the gravity of the charge. At this juncture the analogy to plea bargaining is blatant: by changing one's behavior, which is tantamount to admitting there may have been something offensive in their recent conduct, one hopes to elicit a reduced sentence (treatment that is appreciably less harsh and judgmental).

From a psychoanalytic point of view, it could be said that the act of rejection induces in the recipient a regressive, transferential revival and enactment of the psyche's infantile dread of superego condemnation. In such a state of mind, the person, as though under a spell, cannot help but empower the rejecter and unconsciously scheme to ingratiate a now wounded self with someone typically experienced as a tyrannical parent. What Freud once said in <u>Mourning and Melancholia</u> (1915)--concerning a pathologically bereaved ego that, feeling so unloved, gives up and thinks it is going to die--applies to the aftermath of rejection: the recipient unconsciously believes a part of his self is going to die unless, somehow, the other's malignant judgment is reversed.

In spite of the fact that it engenders an obsessive, painful dependency, the act of rejection for a number of reasons can also be morbidly seductive. There is its apparent finality. It occurs and no apologies are given, no court of appeals is available. There is its intrinsic ambivalence: on the one hand it is obviously subjective and keenly motivated, and on the other hand it seems impersonal, authoritarian, even governmental. The alarming lack of interest in mutuality and empathy is reminiscent of a highly critical parental superego that seems utterly scornful of the adult status of the other. It is not uncommon then for the person to feel they are being treated as though they had no rights, scant conscience, and were little better than a criminal or wayward child. And it is, of course, simultaneously frightening, demoralizing and outrageous that someone--who has only been authorized to perform circumscribed functional duties--can upon a whim, and with seeming impunity, begin to behave as judgmentally and haughtily as a governmentally empowered federal prosecutor. It then seems that only radical withdrawal from any empathic understanding of and complete contempt for the person could ever entitle the other to be so openly condemning. From that perspective it is not surprising that part of the odd devotion to the rejecting object is in order to conduct a secret research project to find out if there is any grain of truth to the horrid charges that have been raised against the self.

DYNAMICS OF A POWER STRUGGLE

Whenever there is a disequilibrium of leverage, status or privilege, as there so often is, the condition is ripe for an eventual power struggle. I have gone into

Dennis' encounter with the token booth clerk in some detail because I think it shows with particular clarity the dynamics of this kind of interaction, one that is played out daily millions of times by people and between people:

Typically, it is initiated by the contemptuous reduction of the solicitor--someone in the disadvantageous position of having to ask for special consideration from another who is empowered to grant or decline the request--to the status of gadfly, a person whose only significance is his nuisance value. What is intrinsically transactional has thereby been converted into a solitary preoccupation with narcissistic gratification. And since the needs of the other are regarded as too insubstantial to be taken into account, there is no legitimate conflict, at least none that is acknowledged. Instead, there is an immediate attack, designed to put the other on the defensive by making him feel as though he is being irrational and unconscionable to assert his wants. The implicit assumption that there is a world of difference between the authenticity of the needs of the one who is exercising power and the one who is soliciting a favor is sufficiently demoralizing and infantalizing so as to be inherently intimidating. For this reason, analogous to how quickly a desire for intimacy can be killed off at its inception, it is extremely easy not only to turn down, but to squash the hope of someone who is requesting something from a person in power. Since someone with authority can be rejecting and cold-hearted with relative impunity, it follows that the other, knowing this and understandably reluctant to provide unnecessary incentive for additional rejections, will be careful to frame any request for special consideration in language that is regarded as appropriately deferential. More to the point, he will tend to be wary of complaining when help is refused, even when inwardly it is regarded as grossly unfair.

The sense that the one who is soliciting is ipso facto in a poor position to assert or defend his rights will reinforce whatever prior feelings of unworthiness he may have. Indeed, every frank entreaty for assistance carries psychic significance: signalling that the power of the one in charge--as well as the comparative powerlessness of the other who, by urgently asking for something, thereby admits he cannot do it for himself--has just been acknowledged.

For all of these reasons, it follows the use of power simultaneously deters corrective feedback in a majority of cases and from that simple dynamic much of the oft-noted abuse of power flows. Put another way, inasmuch as the exercise of power is a process in which reciprocal interaction and corrective feedback play almost no role, there is little to curtail the temptation to extend one's customary field of advantage beyond its legitimate boundaries. The primary thing, of course, which could act as a check on such abuse of power would be an empathic identification with the needs of the other and that, ironically, is just what the aspiring power broker characteristically lacks.

To curry a favor, analogous to asking a question, is to unconsciously signify a clear lack. By contrast, power is forever calling attention to what it has, what it is, in short, to its fullness. It points to what it has accomplished in the past, what it stands for in the present, but not to the future. Its attitude toward time is arrogant: there is no need for change, certainly none necessitated by the present interaction; the only need for change that will be considered is one that it independently decides upon (it is never the situation that the other is raising that will affect or ameliorate the existing power structure). Instead, what is important, what sets things in motion are the rules, the agenda, the stipulation and not feelings and the idiosyncratic wishes of individuals. It therefore does not relate--it regulates, governs or executes what it is certain has to be done. No small part of its ability to intimidate is its posture of never having run into anything it hasn't seen before, that scares it, that it can't handle, or that it can learn from. The implication, clearly, is that the raison d'etre of power transcends the here and now petty world of contingent, specific human need.

A common way to exercise power and restrict the field of action of the other, is to deny whatever request they are making. But in order to do that, one must refuse to acknowledge that any intermediate zone exists in which they can productively interact, i.e., one stubbornly maintains the narrowest possible description of one's duties--typified by the classic disclaimer "that's not my job". The exercise of power, therefore, traditionally suggests that the time for negotiation, which may have existed in the past, is definitely over. Now something has to be done. One of the strongest proofs that someone is in charge, therefore, is the ability to be interpersonally defining: to say, in effect, this is what the situation between us is, this is the way things are. It does this by showing almost no interest in the opinion, the response or perspective of the other, the message being there is to be only one perspective and one interpretation. By thus denying there is anything about which to relate, it is free to nip in the bud anything the other says. It thereby becomes comparatively easy to establish a superior vantage point by simply defining anything the other expresses which is in disagreement as either oppositionalism, irrational behavior or a failure to understand.

Someone in a position of power will typically assert her authority by insisting on a lack of equality: i.e., by taking every opportunity, especially when challenged, to underscore what is objectively unequal about the situation and specifically inferior about the other's vantage point, whether it be the other's lack of experience, technical knowledge or basic intelligence. From a psychodynamic standpoint, it is easy to see that to have power is to be able, with impunity, to unconsciously project one's disavowed vulnerability, ignorance and weakness onto the other. And although a show of power will not manifestly claim infallibility, it will characteristically seek to hide whatever chinks it has in its armor. It therefore does its best not to offer any encouragement that it is about to change its mind or that it could be mistaken. (It is particularly loathe to admit, "I've never seen that before.")

It follows the opportunistic use of power is intrinsically undemocratic. While it does not exactly deny this, it prefers to justify the superior advantage it claims for itself by asserting that its dominance has been attained within a supposedly objective hierarchy of observable skills and performances.

RELATIONSHIP TO THE DEMOCRATIC WAY OF LIFE

In a democracy, it could be said, everyone is afforded an equal chance to be unequal, and thereby prove they are better than someone else. Typically, someone who wields power, especially corporate power, will bolster his belief in the principles of democracy with the assumption that he ascended to his present prestigious position solely on the basis of merit. In other words, it is fair that he has accumulated power because he earned it. And if the means of advancement were fair, then the end result, the pinnacle that was finally scaled, must be considered to have been deserved. This kind of everyday non-sociopathic power--social, professional, business, political--thus claims that it is just power, the implication being that it can therefore exercise its leverage with a relatively clear conscience.

The classic comeback, and counter-argument against this, of course, is that the person is really a bully who is taking unfair advantage of his position regardless of how fairly he has gained it. It follows that the one on the receiving end will be extremely susceptible to a paranoid feeling of being abused. This is because, first of all, it is hard to be able to summon one's better judgment when one feels manipulatively outmanned by the superior resources of the other. And someone who sees himself as having no choice but to subject himself to the influence of the other because of a perceived power differential, typically does not feel good about what he is doing. Since it is almost impossible not to feel pressured if one is acting the way one is because of a fear of the consequences of challenging the other's authority, it is all too easy to suspect (and then project) that one is being intentionally pressured. And if one feels pressured, one also feels disrespected. For why else would the other resort to power, even if he had it, unless he did not trust the person's ability to act freely in a mutually beneficial way. The wielding of power perceived as the use of force is therefore unconsciously equated with a fundamental disbelief in the value of the autonomous self of the person. Furthermore, the use of force implies a lack of concern for the capacity of the person to successfully resist the use of force, to punish the other for the use of force or to be stimulated to resort to force himself. Thus, the implicit assumption when power is being aggressively exercised is that it flows one way, from the top down. When there is resistance, it is usually considered inconsequential, an obstacle to be managed and circumvented, but not feared.

The recipient, therefore, tends to feel paranoid because:

1.   It is hard to appreciate the benign aspects of an other who is perceived to be acting in an unjustifiably coercive fashion.

2.   It is hard to feel one can have a meaningful impact on an other who is relying upon force. After all, what can he contribute or offer--except compliance?

3.   It is hard to believe that--if one does comply and even if it was deemed necessary to do so--one will not be frustrated afterwards. Someone who senses he is being externally compelled to work against his own desires (he would

prefer not to do what he is doing, but is afraid not to) cannot help but feel he has come under the sway of an alien but stronger will. It is natural, then, to both doubt one's own ability to act autonomously, especially when one is being pressured to conform, as well as the underlying intentions of the other: i.e., only a malign parent, bully or an office tyrant would choose to make someone do what they really don't want to do and which does not seem to be in their best interests. By contrast, someone who is genuinely and empathically well-intentioned would at least try to negotiate first and reluctantly use force only as a last resort. Yet, it is a notorious sign of power that force is quickly resorted to as soon as it encounters appreciable resistance. Which, of course, reinforces the suspicion that the power player is a secret bully looking for an opportunity to flex his muscles.

4.   And, finally, for all of these reasons, it is almost impossible to feel respected. It is obvious if one really was respected, the other, as already mentioned, would not have found it necessary to resort to force and even if the person was not respected but was perceived as powerful enough to negate and retaliate in kind to any show of force--power would not have been exercised. Thus, a double narcissistic injury has been sustained: the self has not been respected and the capacity of the self to protect and assert is natural right to autonomously express itself has also not been respected.

It is worth noting how the recipient reacts to a power play. Typically, afterwards, there is no immediate overt response. Someone who feels overpowered usually does not feel worthy or confident enough to engineer a confrontation with their oppressor. On the contrary, there is the nagging sense they either have not earned or have forfeited their right to stand behind what they believe. So instead they ruminate, go through the motions of pretending everything is the same as before, and wait to be alone to figure out what they may have unwittingly done that could ever have provoked or deserved such painful and shabby treatment.

Someone who is thus stimulated to fantasize about immediate retaliation, yet feels powerless to do anything about it, usually does not notice that any possibility of generative intimate contact has been foreclosed. Yet, perhaps the greatest and most destructive fallout for parties who play power games is that the hope of nurturance--without even being mourned in the slightest--has been instantly lost. And this is because it seems so right, so eminently practical to abandon interest in empathic interrelating and focus instead on the machinations of power.

"I'M THE BOSS.
I'M THE BOSS."

In a touching scene occurring at the end of Martin Scorcese's classic film concerning contemporary violence, <u>Raging Bull</u>, Jake Lamota, the former middle weight champion of the world, begins to pace within the narrow confines of his seedy dressing room. Well past his prime as an authentic ring great, in disgrace in boxing circles because of his confession that he once agreed to fix a fight for the mob, having already served a prison term for corrupting the morals of a young girl, he is desperately trying to parlay his tainted celebrity status into a second career as a small-time night club performer. To psych himself up he begins to shadow box in his dressing room, crouching and throwing flurries of vicious body punches for which he was once famous in the ring, chanting out loud between grunts, in a kind of pugilistic mantra of self-empowerment, "I'm the boss. I'm the boss." It is the glaring discrepancy between the grandiosity of his self image and the manifest sleaziness of his current existence that make the scene so poignant.

In the everyday world this theme of being number one, of showing who's in charge--graphically epitomized in the professional prizefighter's do-or-die violent fight for survival--has infiltrated itself in many guises into the fabric of our society. Perhaps the most common example, and the arena for asserting or for having to submit to the realities of rank, power and prestige, is the workplace. Indeed, so interminable are the narcissistic injuries which stem from the basic fact that one has to coexist daily with one's boss, that it is easy to forget, even for a psychotherapist, that beneath their prosaic, repetitive exterior can lie great psychic pain.

It was Lucy, of all my patients, who taught me this. Although she had originally come into therapy in order to recuperate from the termination of a long and unhappy marriage, it quickly became apparent that what most tormented her was the almost continual threat of humiliation she experienced while working as a copy writer in a medium-sized advertising agency. Unlike many patients who channel, discharge and transform unconscious anxiety into an assuaging network of reality-tested complaints, Lucy was acutely aware of her own fragilities, her propensity to take the slightest rebuff to heart, her great need for someone to appreciate, pay attention and be kind to her which she regarded as a compensatory defense, an antidote to her toxic, inaccessible "refrigerator" mother whom she could not help but compare with her good internal parent, her therapist of the preceding five years who had died very suddenly after being diagnosed with lung cancer.

Furthermore, in spite of the fact that a considerable portion of therapy was spent on an extended exploration of Lucy's mistrust, which sometimes bordered on interpersonal paranoia--intensified no doubt by the recent traumatic death of her former therapist--I was often struck with what appeared to be her uncanny instinct to ferret out the manipulative intention of others, usually well before they themselves were conscious of it. Thus, if she were out of the office for several hours and telephoned wanting to know if there had been any messages for her, and the secretary greeted her with "What's up?", she felt disrespected. Should I ask her what constituted the disrespect, without missing a best she would patiently and thoughtfully explicate: secretaries know it is their job to log potentially important messages; are aware or should be that employees who have been out of the office are appropriately curious as to whether anyone has tried to contact them in their absence; and are therefore creating an unnecessary obstacle by feigning puzzlement as to the purpose of her call. According to Lucy, such an act was hostile. By disowning responsibility and putting the ball in her court, the implication was that she had yet to justify the need for contact and was thereby on the brink of becoming an intrusion on their time. To do that, however, it would be necessary first to obviate the history of their relationship: supposedly founded on cooperative interaction in the service of a common functional goal--and to deny what little part they shared, would be to take something that typically was intrinsically impersonal and make it even more so.

Lucy was equally unforgiving when it came to receptionists who did not always exchange morning salutations, to co-workers who, envious of her ability, seemed eager to undermine her performance, to advertising clients who considered it their due to be deferred and catered to regularly. Not surprisingly, she was almost morbidly sensitive to what she regarded as the stock-in-trade but infuriatingly petty mind games of her boss, the firm's senior copy writer, and a man who often called upon his Master's degree in psychology in order to penetrate people's coverups to their underlying hidden agendas. Thus, whenever a bone of contention arose between them--the fact that she was one of the lowest paid employees in the company, that her best work generally went unnoticed, that, despite her obvious talent and enthusiastic hard work, she had made no discernible advancement in the four years she had been there--her boss, cognizant of her sensitive nature and manifest insecurity, after dutifully hearing Lucy out, would cunningly eye her and with a savvy, patronizing smile, inquire, "Could this be a trust issue, on your part?"

Which of course maddened Lucy and caused her to endlessly wonder aloud in session after session how she had ever landed in such a prison of a job and when she would ever be liberated? And as her therapist I could not help but be struck by what fertile soil employer-employee relations was for engendering feelings of abuse and neglect or for fanning flickering flames of self-doubt and self-hate.

So I had to concur with Lucy that the boss, after all, has the power. He does not have to explain himself, to initiate contact, to relate in any meaningful way if he does not want to. Whatever interactions do take place, are ultimately subject to his overriding interpretation. To a considerable extent employee behavior is initiated by his orders--not, as is more customary, by autonomous unconscious desire or spontaneous transactional stimulus. Although there is token deference to the value of feedback, there is only one interpersonal perspective that matters. The relationship as such is based on how efficiently each party can manage, if not outright exploit the resources of the other: i.e., the employee's resources for the purpose of increasing productivity, the boss's resources (wages) in order to accumulate capital. The transaction is therefore one of instrumentality. It follows, feedback, from the perspective of the boss, is result-oriented and pragmatic--not to know more about the self of the other, but to gather information concerning the other's responses which are viewed as means to ends. While the self of the person may be noted, it is usually seen as either a potential obstacle or ally, but rarely as something worthy of being encountered on its own terms.

In sum, what is chilling about transactions based on power is the extent to which intimacy and relational needs almost instantly are made to appear irrelevant: as though there is a parallel psychic universe of only power operations--where all non-intimate issues are to be resolved by force--that lies at hand and into which we readily may move whenever the unconscious need is strong enough. It might be asked how the possibility for intimacy could be so swiftly blotted out in a transactional world based on personal advantage and leverage? Part of the answer is that the birth of intimacy, a complex but exceedingly fragile process, is easily aborted by even a half-hearted show of rejection (think of how a single cold look from a stranger who up until then had seemed genuinely beguiling, can effectively annihilate any hope of a meaningful encounter). Since a power play is characteristically perceived as a decisive rejection of the other, it will automatically suppress any prior need to relate and because, as mentioned, there is an unconscious recognition that when there is intimacy power will be used as a last resort (and vice versa), the typical reaction of the other to a transaction based on power--such as a boss giving an order--will be an initial shock that one's need for autonomy is being so summarily discounted.

In that case, the psychodynamic reaction is likely to be:

1.   The person tries to cover up her immediate resentment at being given what is considered a demeaning directive with a nervous display of false compliance (e.g., "Sure").

2.   Usually, the person's self-esteem has been wounded by the perceived rebuff and she is therefore too demoralized to assert her need to be treated with greater respect. In her weakened ego state, it seems much too risky, as well as potentially embarrassing, to confront her present conflict over a lack of mutuality. Instead, the temptation is to deny that one has been narcissistically injured by identifying with both the task at hand--compliantly carrying out what one has just been ordered to do--and the need to do it (reminding oneself, consciously and unconsciously, that the censure of the boss is something that has to be avoided).

3.   It all adds up, of course, to an endless deferment of underlying personal issues. This is classically seen in boss-employee relationships where traditionally the most honest communication occurs when someone either quits or gets fired: i.e., when the onus of performance pressure is lifted and the person is comparatively free to express his true feelings.

THE BRUSH-OFF

Of all the mind games Lucy felt subject to given her status as a hard-working, gifted but unempowered employee, none was as exasperating to her as "the brush-off". She defined this as instances when her boss not only did not respect her, but made no real attempt to even understand or make sense of what she was saying. On such occasions she often felt that his lack of simple comprehension was so gross that it could not be unintentional. No, she reasoned, it must be the product of an unconscious parody by her boss of how she was expressing herself: by reducing her usually earnest and well-rehearsed thoughts to something that was either supposedly immediately obvious or a plain non-sequitur he was in effect infantalizing her by implying, "You think you mean this, but what you are really saying is . . .". But then, of course, she would wonder if she were being paranoid? (She realized that if her boss thought there was any reason she would grudgingly but silently submit to his brush-offs other than that she was terrified not to--then he surely must think she was stupid.)

As I listened to this, I had been reading Christopher Bollas' great essay, "The Function of History" (1995) in which he discussed what he termed "the hit of the fact", especially the cumulative effect of external trauma to create a caesura in the self, a blank state that would freeze the creative elaboration of significant related thoughts and feelings. And I wondered, following this, if, at bottom, what is so frightening about the unambiguous exercise of power is that it blindly converts a living inter-psychic experience into a fact: i.e., it refuses to consider the experiential interchange as viable and capable of growth (which is why there is often a residual suffocating feeling of having been psychically buried alive).

In short, as personified by the quintessential American boss, the bearer of power behaves as though everything he needs to know, he knows. He is only concerned with acts. In a crude Sartrian sense (1956) you could say he unconsciously considers himself a low-grade, corporate existentialist, someone who is defined by his actions, who has a proven ability to not only be concrete but to leave concrete effects in his wake. And this can be truly disturbing to others who typically are unaccustomed to defining themselves through their deeds. In no small measure, therefore, the identity--I am a person who has power--derives from a capacity to make an impact on another.

It follows power ceases to exist, is emasculated as soon as it becomes or appears to be dysfunctional. In this respect, it is unconsciously equated with orgasmic potency: there is no in between, one is either potent or impotent. It is obvious such an either/or perspective puts tremendous pressure on the person to perform which in turn can engender in the other a paranoia that it will be hard to dissuade someone intent upon wielding power from achieving their aims (if only because it is perceived that failure is tantamount to having done something shameworthy).

Unconsciously, therefore, the impulse for power strives to express itself in the guise of potency. Whenever it is manifestly swollen and primed for discharge, it should do so expeditiously without letting anything delay it. The implication is that once it is faced with a stimulus and situation calling for some sort of decisive action, it can respond as though by second nature, instinctively and naturally. It does not need to pause to think. Someone, therefore, who intends to exercise power does not want to reveal any telltale signs of a lack of confidence, uncertainty or tentativeness. When there is an underlying insecurity, as there invariably is to a greater or lesser extent, this will manifest itself as a rush to premature closure, the unconscious strategy being to push the transaction into the past tense as quickly as possible. It follows that one of the most upsetting things to the recipient of a power play is this residual sense of an interaction that is very much alive, psychically present, open-ended and in process being treated as something final and over with: an historical fact. To put it another way, the use of power, when it is a primary substitute for interrelating, reifies the self of the other.

MARKETING THE SELF

To a definite extent, advertising, marketing and sales are beholden--when it comes to motivating people--to a philosophy of power. After all, motivating people through advertising really means discovering and then utilizing the power necessary to get others to respond in the way that you want; while marketing seems based on the believe that people can be driven by subliminal stimuli to overcome their natural ability to sensibly say no; and selling can be boiled down to the assembling of interpersonal points of leverage that operate principally to your advantage. All three share the pessimistic conclusion that you do not get anything anywhere through the act of revealing yourself, communicating with or trusting the other. You only get somewhere through managing and manipulating your impressions (Goffman, 1959), through finding and consolidating an opportunistic power base. In this cynical world, what Winnicott (1960) has referred to as a true self is only one more commodity to be bartered.

My own interest in the arts of persuasion and coercion, of compulsively looking for an edge, of buying and selling, go back a long way. In high school, a favorite teacher had taught us, as he saw it, from the idealistic vantage point of a passionate Democrat, the evolution of the American consumer's attitude toward big business. In the beginning that attitude had been decidedly anti-business, influenced by the awareness of outrages committed by people like the first Rockefeller and the so-called original "robber barons" of the late nineteenth century. Acknowledging the problem, American industry set out in earnest to develop what was a revolutionary idea in the early twentieth century, embodied in the buzzword "public relations": intended to counteract the widespread view of American businessmen as predators upon the public, it was boosted by a second buzzword--the concept of "public service". Accordingly, as the twentieth century unfolded, American business began slowly but persistently to promote the idea that everything they do is somehow done for the benefit of the American consumer.

Since I had grown up accepting the idea (not that I especially believed it) that businessmen exist to serve the public, the revelation that such a claim might be little more than a duplicitous pose or expedient strategy was fascinating. Yet in retrospect, what is even more astonishing, in the face of nearly universal cynicism, is the degree to which this sanitized image of the American businessman is still taken for granted: at the time of this writing (1996) it shows no signs of abatement.

This is not, by the way, to imply a deprecatory view of salesmen per se; it is meant, instead, to call attention to the relationship they have been professionally enlisted to foster. If the dynamic hallmark of that relationship, as is tireless alleged, is really public-spirited service, then that means a definite caring and nurturing predisposition of mind must exist *prior* to the initial contact with a customer (who by definition must be a stranger). Yet simple reflection will show that true nurturance and cultivation of another's needs is a relatively advanced and delicate interpersonal transaction, and therefore almost always comes after a personal relationship has been established, hardly ever before. Unless, of course, the prototypical salesman happens to be the kind of individual who has been characterized as an especially empathic, or what is sometimes called therapeutic, personality: that is, one who has the capacity and talent to begin a relationship with a complete stranger by wisely and sensitively resonating with his needs. Yet even psychotherapists--for whom a therapeutic personality is supposedly a requisite tool of the trade--are rarely equipped, in my experience, with such a benevolent temperament.

How then can stock-in-trade salesmen, who as we know are chosen for their aggressive and proven pursuit of profitable self-advancement, ever live by such an egoless ideal as serving the public? It is a simple truth that they cannot, but it was drummed into me through working, over the past ten years, with struggling artists, who, thinking they were merely detouring and regrouping in a temporary, stop-gap job, found themselves mired in that contemporary telemarketing sweatshop, a "boiler room".

It is my thesis that the boiler room, admittedly the underbelly and canker of large-scale corporate business, can tell us much about the respectable superstructure that smugly squats on top of it. This may be because the boiler room--analogous to the way psychosis or mental breakdown, although comparatively rare, traditionally reveals volumes about what goes on underneath the more sedate, seamless covers of the well-coordinated personality--in its unabashed, unbridled greed may dramatize what lies concealed beneath the unctuous business pretense of serving the public.

Over forty years ago an unassuming light comedy, A Letter To Three Wives (a film that has since become a classic), starring Kirk Douglas and Ann Southern, made its debut. In it Kirk Douglas plays a disgruntled, underpaid school teacher who conceives of himself as a passionate lover of pure literary values, and who is revolted at what he apprehends as the engulfing tidal wave of sleazy and philistine American advertising, ironically spearheaded by his wife's enterprising marketing firm. In what seemed at the time a stock melodramatic speech, Douglas lashes out at advertisers who glorify their products as not only the best, but as the solution to life's most enduring hardships.

What is remarkable after forty years is how well that speech stands up, since it in no way was meant to be prophetic, but was simply dished up as entertainment, as contemporary slick movie dialogue. And while it is true that today's advertising is often presented tongue in cheek, the message seems clear: objects are of comparable, perhaps even greater, importance than people or relationships. What advertising, marketing, and sales all promote, instead of the interpersonal relationship, is what might be called an objective relationship to the primary objects in one's immediate inanimate environment. What is attractive is the product, and what salesmen, accordingly, are primarily promoting is the *charisma of the product.* In sales, what is omnipotent is not the person but the product, and it follows that advertisements often depict human beings as being either seduced by it or under its spell.

Seen in this way, the psychology of sales is an attempt to excite the prospective buyer similarly to the way that the seducer tries to arouse the person to be seduced. Analogous to the moment of truth when the seducer (as for example in a disguised sexual seduction) frankly reveals his intent, the "close" in a well-thought-out sales pitch is carefully deferred until the buyer is believed to be optimally primed. Such behavior strongly suggests that the salesman, like the seducer, does not believe that anyone would buy his product unless he or she were sold on it first.

In this sense, selling can only be a manipulation, and the salesman can get what he wants only by hiding what he is really asking for. It follows that the salesman will relate to the buyer essentially through the product, and the buyer in turn will respond primarily through the expression of a positive or negative reaction to the proffered product-stimulus. This is a triangular relationship characterized by indirectness: one that is based solely on need and not on the person, or even the hope of intimacy. The only question, the whole point of the relationship, is whether or not an isolated need will be satisfied. The underlying assumption of sales appears to be that people are needy in a greedy way, and that when the targeted need is patiently and skillfully gratified, they are more likely than not to be seduced into buying. Since it is assumed that customers in general want as much as they can get while giving as little as possible and since salesmen have been conditioned to make as much profit as possible at the lowest possible costs, there is an uneasy awareness that the real relationship, if the ulterior motives were candidly acknowledged by both parties, will necessarily be combative and incongruent.

To dissolve the stalemate or potential escalation of such conflicting needs, the myth has been cultivated that what the salesman really wants is to service, and not sell to the customer. It is important that no matching myth has been fashioned, which would be that what the customer really wants is to service the salesman, for example, by sponsoring and endorsing his product--which, when you think of it, is no less believable than the reverse. It is hardly an accident, then, that the hypothetical consumer, by implication and omission, is encouraged to think that he will be indulged in the very best service the salesman can offer, with no obligation whatsoever to reciprocate. A picture is thereby deliberately drawn of the captivated buyer as someone who is not only free unselfconsciously to pig out on his favorite product, but who will be admired for doing so.

This portrait of the buyer as put forward by the seller, is suggestive of the addict: but here the supposed addiction is to the product. And there is a sense, analogous to the parallel processes of seduction and addiction, in which it can be said that the salesman operates, or tries to, on a similar principle: to proceed through a series of intentionally small, nonthreatening steps to an orchestrated euphoria, with the expected toxic side effects (inability to handle payments or beneficially to utilize the product) deftly deferred. This is why salesmen talk only about product benefits, and why a sales pitch can be seen as a kind of seduction, which, when it succeeds, does so for comparable reasons. The subject is led down the garden path, tantalized by one harmless pleasure (product benefit) after another, until a mood of appetitive arousal is reached, at which point the "close" is attempted, to elicit money for something that until then had appeared almost effortlessly accessible. The salesman, like the seducer, tries to lull the buyer's understandable fear that he is the target of aggressive greed by pretending to be himself under the spell (the seducer's flattery) of an overriding wish to provide service; in other words, he is not there to take, he is there to give.

It is therefore hardly surprising that salesmen, again like seducers, will measure the potency of their persuasive powers by stacking it up against the weight of the customer's resistance. Great salesmen, like Don Juans, love to boast how they overcame seemingly impossible challenges (the diehard customer as equivalent to the virgin), and to that extent their relationships bear a nonreciprocal, predator-prey stamp. In place of communication, there is the art of misdirection and persuasion. Instead of negotiating and working things out in a spirit of mutuality, there is a determination to blot out resistance and "overcome" objections. There is also the parallel between the seduced one's retrospective sense of having shamefully participated in a corrupt, self-compromising act, and what has been called "buyer's remorse," typically occurring within forty-eight hours after the sale, when the customer figures out that he has overextended himself and not acted in his own best interest.

For all of these reasons, the underlying conception of human nature that guides the psychology of selling can be likened to a cartoon, yet one, despite the just-kidding, tongue-in-cheek disclaimers of most advertising, that deserves to be taken seriously because it says much about the sales mind, and could be fairly described as reductionism run amok. In this view, people are seen as creatures with instinctual behavioral buttons that, pressed by the appropriate motivational or subliminal stimulus, will "release" their programmed appetitive response.

Once again the question deserves to be asked: What kind of human being is it whose mood is profoundly elevated by mere proximity to a preferred product? The answer seems to be, one who is psychologically impaired, with a marked deficit of imaginative inner life, and who is therefore fixated on objects at hand. There is a remarkable similarity between this notion of human nature and that of lower animals (e.g., birds and fish) as developed by the ethologists Konrad Lorenz (1970, 1971) and Niko Tinbergen (1951): the concept of fixed action pattern, the IRM (innate releasing mechanism, a genetically programmed behavior pattern, constituted by a few key behaviors or a few principal behavioral strategies, which are triggered into play by the activation of a sign stimulus) and the releasers. In humans, from the vantage point of advertising, the IRM can be likened to an appetite for any product ever designed by a manufacturer, and the "releaser" is an image or association that effectively triggers it. Once the releaser (e.g., the shape of a car) is activated, the fixed action pattern is set in motion, so the scenario goes, and the consumer is driven to purchase and find satisfaction in the object of his desire. It is no accident that advertisements often portray the consumer as ravenous, an animal enjoying its prey, and accordingly, depict the ego of the typical customer as ludicrously weak, not to be respected, but to be dealt with through learning how to surmount objections, while the superego is relegated to the aforementioned simplistic category of "buyer's remorse".

Such a view of human nature is close to a caricature of the original psychoanalytic model of man as primarily a creature driven by id (instinct), and it carries definite implications. As such the pitch, like the seduction, is a strategy that assumes that people are programmed according to primary needs that have to be met, and that in order to ensnare the target, it is necessary to tap into the opportune impulse. A pitch and a seduction share a deep pessimism concerning the possibility of safely, honestly, and intimately having one's needs responded to: and it follows that their intrinsic manipulation will be the antithesis of what is called symbiosis, in which surviving alone is seen as impossible. By contrast, success in sales, as in seduction (although this is routinely denied), is predicated on the impossibility of surviving together: the zero-sum belief that to the victor belong the spoils.

We began this chapter on the fringe with the sociopath and ended with something as mundanely American as the salesman, two examples of how power is used or rather abused. In the next chapter we explore in greater depth some of the underlying dynamics and strategies of what are often experienced--and cynically explained away--as just power plays.

CHAPTER TWO
Power Plays
"YOUR CREDENTIALS ARE AT THE BOTTOM OF THE TOTEM POLE"

In the two years that I had known her, Marlene had often recreated the scene in which her supervisor had delivered that dreadful pronouncement on her lack of qualifications for the job at hand. As an intern working towards her masters degree in social work she was dependent upon at least a nominal approval from the executive director of the local bureau of child welfare, a no-nonsense, unmarried woman who was proud of her reputation for being difficult and who seemed to relish supervising and teaching the ropes to overly zealous graduate students who may have thought they had little to learn. Marlene did not mind the gross unfairness of the evaluation--she was generally recognized to be among the very best in her class--the obvious attempt to put her in her place and the apparent utter disinterest in her future development nearly as much as what she perceived as its undisguised tone of flat-out contempt.

And try as she would, in spite of the insight she sometimes achieved in therapy into her deep-rooted susceptibility to a variety of narcissistic injuries, she was able neither to forgive nor forget what her supervisor had said. Her dilemma was that something in the core of her self had found it imperative, yet extremely hard if not impossible, to challenge such open contempt. For it seemed especially frightening to Marlene that anyone, regardless of the authority invested in them or their position, could dare to be so wounding--as though utterly unafraid of the capacity of the other to retaliate. To first create such monumentally hurt feelings in the other, and then proceed to act indifferently to her handiwork, as her supervisor had done, could not help but elicit a paranoid response: if the person fails so miserably when it comes to understanding how they have gratuitously damaged us, how are they ever going to be motivated to make contact with our true self?

Furthermore, the implication of their insolent, judgmental tone is that the object of their contempt is also the sole cause of it. That they deserve official censure, therefore, is irrefutable and does not merit further consideration. A large part of its punitive impact can be attributed to this indifference to time or process, with its implicit assumption that something as complicated and polysemous as a self can be reduced and encapsulated in something as unidimensional as a contemptuous opinion. Once again the other is typically thrown into disarray and left to ruminate how is it possible that such psychical disfiguring could take place? A common initial reaction is to wonder if somehow a mistake has been made or if one has unwittingly needlessly provoked the other. Usually denial quickly sets in and takes the form that the expression of outright contempt must be a defensive reaction and cannot be an honest mistake. When no such acknowledgment, however, is forthcoming, which is characteristically the case, the other may begin to suspect that, unbeknownst to them, some truly horrible part of their self may be showing. Such considerations, of course, are especially disturbing because regardless of how self-scathing or critical one may be, there is an immense difference between lodging an internal complaint that a certain aspect of one's behavior may be despicable and hearing essentially the same thing from the lips of another.

For no matter how penetrating, a self-critique is always only one among many inner voices, some of which, if only partially, will value and support the self. Furthermore, being hard on oneself can always be seen as an attempt at constructive criticism or, at the worst, as the administration of a deserved self-reproach. In both cases, there is the additional mitigating circumstance that one's conscience, by being privy to so much psychic data, is incomparably more objective than that of an outsider and to that extent even self-hate can feel more like an act of justice than any so-called impartial external judgment. We can see that one can learn to live with internal condemnation provided one thinks that it is somewhat fair and emanates from the same source, that in more propitious circumstances, is capable of affirming the value of the true self. There is then at least the hope that if one mends one's ways the approval of one's conscience can be regained. And even if one's inner voice continues to chastise, there is the consolation it does so in part because of what it knows and has seen and not because it hates and is out for blood (in spite of how abusive one's parental introject may be). Also, since whatever moral judgment is delivered comes from a part of the self, there is always the possibility that an appeal--the appellate court judge, after all, is you--can be successful. Depending on how desperately besieged one feels, one can force a particularly unbearable negative inner voice to listen endlessly to psychic defense arguments: the equal time rule in this case can be dispatched with impunity in a way that it never can with an outsider.

By contrast, there is often the sense--when it is the other who is being brazenly contemptuous--that an irreversible sentence has been passed which may never be brought up again let alone challenged. What is instead required in order to restore oneself is nothing less than changing the behavioral self of an oppositional other as compared to altering one's internal perspective. The realization that it is impossible for the other to have nearly as extensive a basis for a serious personal critique as you yourself can provide contributes to the impression that one has just been morally indicted, tried and convicted without the benefit of a fair trial. Even someone who has a long history of being condemned within the court of their own conscience--a depressive personality, for example--can nevertheless, when necessary, conduct a counter trial of sorts, can raise defending introjects and try to force the punitive part of one's mind to at least partially listen. If all else fails, one can attempt to drown out the negative voice in one's head with a deluge of defensive arguments.

It is just this one cannot do when the reproach comes from the mind of another, if only because the expulsive force of the contempt makes it clear that no psychic space will be allowed for a differing and more nourishing representative of one's self. It follows, for all of these reasons, that the recovery time for a narcissistic injury incurred by a toxic introject is generally much quicker than is the case for its interpersonal counterpart; and this is due to the fact there are far more coping strategies for diluting the pain such as distracting oneself, drowning out negative voices and so on.

"JUST DO IT"

Matt is a soft-spoken forty-year-old civil engineer who is embarrassed and somewhat dismayed at his rapid descent into ineffectuality whenever he is called upon to discipline his twelve-year-old son. Priding himself on being fair-minded, thoughtful and, above all, decent, he takes it as a personal insult that his son seems to go out of his way to give him a hard time whenever he attempts to inform him it is necessary to do something he apparently doesn't want to do. What he is perhaps most sensitive to is his son's sarcastic accusation that--if challenged in the slightest to provide a rationale for his choice of disciplinary action--the best he could offer was an unintended aping of the famed Nike injunction--"Just do it."

In therapy, Matt had to admit there was a certain cruel truth to his son's campy pop culture parody. For his normal resolve, steadiness of character and predictability of response seemed to vanish whenever he felt obligated to play the disciplinarian. To tell someone what to do, to order them about was one of the most uncomfortable ways to treat another person that he could imagine. Like many even-humored people who are instinctively repelled by the use of force, Matt would do his best to prevent a situation from escalating to that point. If the occasion did arise when he felt compelled to throw his weight around, to be aggressively authoritarian, he hoped it would be understood that he was just trying to get an unpleasant task over with as quickly as possible. When it came to his own son, of course, Matt did more than hope. He fully expected, in gratitude for all that he had done for him, that his son would be an empathic, if subordinate collaborator. To be instead challenged, when he was at his most fragile and in need of an ally, was less than a low blow. It was a sign of the profoundest disrespect.

What he could not see, and what his son saw clearly, was that as soon as resistance was offered to his intent to pull parental rank, Matt quickly resorted to the tactics of the bully. "Just do it" transparently meant "do it or else". From the standpoint of our theme, it is worth noting how often--beneath the implicit authorization to exercise power when necessary conferred by a host of significant parental, social, professional and business roles--lies a stark latent threat.

This element of danger that adds juice to the use of power ranges in intensity from the frankly sociopathic--where someone seems ready at the drop of a hat to do serious harm to the other--to the propensity each of us has to turn bully when sufficiently provoked (e.g., to train a dirty look on anyone who steps on our toes, literally or figuratively).

PSYCHOLOGY OF A THREAT

The implication is that the person has come to the end of his tether--of civilized exchange, of agreeing to disagree--will not tolerate further discomfort and will therefore probably respond to the next provocation with a show of force. How seriously such a threat is regarded will depend on the perception of the context from which it arose. If up until the moment the ultimatum is delivered the person was believed to have been acting reasonably, the threat may be viewed as something that can be weathered. The hope then is that if one simply cuts short the behavior that has seemingly triggered the outbreak of aggression, the person will be placated and restored to their former, more restrained self.

On the other hand, if the context is practically non-existent--if, for example, one has somehow caught a stranger's eye on a train or in the street and almost immediately, in a matter of seconds has received a murderous stare in return--the situation is cause for alarm. Because if someone can come to the end of their tether in the time it takes to exchange glances, how much more provoked will they be if actually embroiled in sustained confrontation? (It is of interest that a number of arguments that end in homicides originated with one of the parties taking offence at the other's real or imagined staring. Robert DeNiro's famous line, as a psychotic taxi driver--"Are you talking to me?"--is a dramatic illustration of the danger of provoking someone with a short fuse, someone who is likely to resort quickly to violence, which is another way of saying that the situation is one in which there is no time to process conflict.)

By contrast, it is obvious that a basis for civilized dispute (of e.g., "let us agree to disagree") is that time has unconsciously been built in for the operation of coping strategies and the tolerant containment and de-escalation of potentially disruptive or frankly traumatizing conflicts. What the threat of the imminent use of force does is to obliterate the ingrained security blanket derived from the belief that benevolent social rules will be applied to whatever instances of inter-psychic tension spontaneously arise. Not surprisingly, the effect then is to produce a panicky sense of being on the brink of psychic anarchy--the state of mind for which policemen were invented and the occasion when the sighting of one is especially welcome.

From this perspective, the so-called masochistic personality is often someone who is only testing the waters: unconsciously trying to elicit a negative response in order to feel that through the act of initiation one thereby gains control, while nursing the faint hope that in lieu of rejection one may receive serendipitous approval. When the reaction instead is a contemptuous or threatening one, the consequences can be even more demoralizing to a masochistically provocative person who may then believe he has found further proof of his worthlessness.

THE MAKINGS OF A GOOD ENFORCER

Although Irene considered herself far too anxious and fearful of retaliation to ever threaten another person, no matter how angry she was, she took undisguised vicarious pleasure in being associated with someone who could, when the occasion warranted it, be effectively intimidating. If that person happened to be her boyfriend, someone who was jealously invested in being her bodyguard as well as her lover, so much the better. In therapy Irene recollected with nostalgic glee the sense of safety and privileged protection she enjoyed in the company of her current boyfriend, a former professional middleweight boxer who was especially proud of the extracurricular knockouts he had accumulated in the street. And she would never forget the thrill she had experienced upon being introduced one afternoon at lunch to Wally, a friend of her boyfriend: a scary-looking giant of a man who had devised his own method for collecting previously uncollectible debts--he would show up unannounced at the delinquent person's home, terrorize them to whatever extent was necessary, and simply refuse to leave until he had payment in hand. As she recounted it, you had only to meet Wally once in the flesh to realize just how feasible his method was.

The kind of enforcer Irene was alluding to, and being titillated by, from the standpoint of our theme, is an extreme, if sociopathic version of the commonplace bully. Although, as has been mentioned, each of us under certain circumstances will endeavor to obtain the lion's share of whatever they are pursuing through intimidating the other, only some of us are especially good at it. As Harry Stack Sullivan (1953) once noted, it is frightening to be aggressively, publicly angry: because of an anxiety instilled by an awareness that things are out of control, that the ante has been raised and a big risk has just been taken which can have serious consequences it if backfires, not surprisingly most people take that risk only when they are pressured to do so, that is, when they feel it has become dangerous to be perceived as civilized and passive.

By contrast, it is characteristic of the bully that not only is he not afraid to be conspicuously angry but that he seems to enjoy the power he obviously has to intimidate others. Instead of hiding or deferring it, therefore, he flaunts it. Since the fabric of social conduct and interpersonal relations at least in our society appears to rest on a concept of fairness, it is unnerving to encounter someone whose modus operandi palpably entails being unfair and who seemingly does not grow anxious, as most of us do, when he is acting in a blatantly antisocial manner. Indeed, instead of tolerating, empathizing with or being supportive and nurturing of the other's perceived social disadvantage, the bully goes out of his way to punish weakness. And to the extent that the bully is viewed as almost a professional aggressor, someone who spends considerably more time than the ordinary person at trying to be threatening, it is assumed they must be good at what they do.

This combination of an aggressive, intolerant, punitive and exploitative attitude towards the next person's weaknesses and fears and an aura of being an experienced and willing combatant, create the bully's required intimidation. Knowing this, they can afford to search out the soft and anxious underbelly of the other's self. Rather than relate they establish dominance and then seek to coerce the other into compliance with and gratification of their needs.

In light of this, our cultural obsession with fairness is a necessary compensating mechanism with which to make the almost infinite power and prestige inequities that permeate the structure of our society more bearable. Another way to say this is that if someone has more power than we do it is imperative that we trust he or she did not acquire it and does not intend to use it deviously. The practice of being fair, as a code of conduct adhered to, therefore tends to alleviate our paranoia that the power the other has will be used to our disadvantage (as it often is).

From this it can immediately be seen that, unconsciously, abusive treatment is equated with an unfair use of power. The bully, thus, is never perceived to be fighting fairly.

WHAT IS A FAIR USE OF POWER?

Power always implies an inequity or disequilibrium of force, psychic or otherwise. When someone's ability to negatively impact on you in any sphere of the self is greater than your ability to defend against such toxic impact, the person is perceived to have power. Such a person can then elicit a distinctly unwanted response--as for example feeling put in one's place, humiliated, bested, restricted, coerced to do something one does not want to do but is afraid not to; or, in a more positive vein, experiencing a tender, vulnerable emotion that one would prefer not to experience (e.g., obsessively desiring and pursuing someone who continues to reject you). Power operations tend to be dynamically specific. Often an abuser can be decidedly weaker in an overall sense than his victim. Thus a small child who perceives he can hurt his parents' feelings by showing sufficient disrespect will also realize the considerable power that comes from being able to disturb a significant other.

By contrast, when power is utilized as a tool in the service of the actualization of the true self or when the emphasis is on the relationship and the reciprocal implementing of human needs, it typically is viewed as being deployed fairly. This, of course, is the antithesis of what occurs when the unconscious aim is narcissistic self-fortification.

What makes belief in the benign use of power so difficult is that there is almost always a certain paranoia that the person is a secret, selfish bully and that any show of fairness is disingenuous. There may also be resentment that even if power is being used fairly, it does not mean much. After all, a person with power is in a winning position and it costs little to be generous about it. Indeed, it may earn credit for future dealings. Which points to the common sense behind the American motto that the real test of a good sport is whether you can be a gracious loser. It follows that the bully--the quintessential example of someone who uses his power in a mean-spirited way--is invariably regarded as a poor loser, par excellence.

The realization that someone has power over you--because you can never be sure as to their covert motivations--creates uneasiness. One can always hide behind the structure of power and because the presence of power will tend to preoccupy the forefront of the other's consciousness (due to its ability to stir up anxiety), it is easy for the self of both parties to become blurred. When a transaction is regarded as a power one, therefore, the other will tend to relate to the dynamics of the perceived power differential and not to the vicissitudes of the underlying self.

This is why, afterwards--when the other tries to reconstruct what just happened from the standpoint of relational issues--there is typically an anxious sense of a blank or void. One does not know if the reason one cannot readily locate the self of the person who has been exerting pressure is because it was not there in the first place or because one was too self-absorbed and defensive at the time to empathize with it.

The roots of the paranoia regarding bearers of power, of course, go back to infancy and the relationship to parents who not only totally dominate, literally holding the power of life and death in their hands, but require and often extort compliance and obedience from their children in order to satisfactorily raise and educate them. Whether it is true that absolute power corrupts absolutely, it is certain that such parental power invariably, to a greater or lesser degree, corrupts; and no one realizes this better than children who are forced to recognize how frequently their parents' use of power--especially at times when there is a clear conflict of interests and issues of discipline are being raised--is patently self-serving and decidedly not for their own good. The child in every adult is thereby haunted by a fear that his parent was a bully (secret if not overt), and unconsciously it must be asked--if the person who supposedly loved and nurtured you more than anyone else in the world was even in some part a bully--how can a stranger with no vested interest in your autonomous existence, not be one also, if ever given the chance?

It was Freud who pointed out how much of psychic development is a direct product of the prolonged biological helplessness of the human infant: first the internalization of parental prohibitions which crystallize into what he called a superego (ego ideal plus conscience) creating in the process a permanent weakness in the ego in relation to authoritarian imagoes; followed by the continued need for dependence in adulthood, as manifested by the universal religious search for a benign cosmic paternalism. It is only a short step from this to substitute in the unconscious powerlessness for helplessness and to see the power which parents indubitably have to safeguard and nurture the child and the power inherited by schools and society at large to train the young adult to not only survive but flourish in the larger, non-familial world as tantamount to holding the power to determine their fate for better or worse. So it may be that we are too readily in awe whenever we perceive ourselves on the short end of a power transaction because it revives in us derivative feelings from our childhood when we were susceptible to being psychically overmatched in almost any interaction in which issues of authority and life experience were at stake.

To the degree that a display of power is unconsciously equated with parental dominance, it becomes difficult to trust the other, to feel secure that we can let down our guard and do not need to assert or reestablish our independence. And a common reaction, therefore, to a feeling of having been dominated is afterwards to anxiously search for and try to reconnect to one's own center of adult power (as though to reassure ourselves that in spite of the setback we really are psychically grown up).

The awe, if not the paranoia, engendered by evidence of the other's power perhaps becomes clearer if we examine our own internal relationship to the psychic structure that we raise to a position of authority over us: our superego. It is worth noting, when it comes to a discussion of the generative aspects of the superego, that the professional literature has comparatively little to say. Instead, the emphasis is squarely on how harsh, punitive or prohibitive the function of the superego is (Christopher Bollas, 1987, is one of the few analysts who writes profoundly about the nurturing ways in which the self may be treated as an object). There are good reasons for this: as therapists we rarely see examples of a generative, benign superego. Nor, it may be added, do we see such sterling examples outside of therapy.

One may therefore ask why--if parents are good enough mothers and good enough fathers and if the prohibitions and rules of being that are laid down accordingly are sufficiently facilitating and empathic-- superegos tend to be so forbidding, remote and generally unforgiving? Think how rare it is that one looks to one's superego for nurturance and collaboration, instead of approval and validations based on performance. The answer I think, although overlooked, is obvious. The prohibitions and rules of being laid down by parents are done so by people who typically are in a state of mind that, bluntly speaking, is punitive and demanding.

While clearly unfortunate from the standpoint of their children's development, it is nevertheless understandable if one looks at the dynamics of parental love and interrelating. The intimacy that exists between parents and children--primarily because of its profoundly non-reciprocal nature--is probably the most demanding and difficult to achieve. In no other type of known relationship is one required to give so much and expect so little back. With one's children, in addition to empathy and love, one is expected to: literally feed, clothe, house, raise, educate, protect and shepherd them through every developmental passage up until adulthood. By contrast, children are not expected to reciprocate like services. More importantly, from the standpoint of intimacy, they are not required to be able to empathize with and nurture the deepest needs of their parents' true selves. (In no small part, of course, this is because parents are characteristically reluctant to acknowledge, let alone show, their more intimate desires to their children.)

It could be said, therefore, that <u>parents love their children before they know them as persons</u>. And it becomes immediately apparent that one of the great differences between parental love and intimacy between consenting adults is that parental love to a considerably greater degree seems to be based on biologically programmed non-reciprocal attachment needs. To put it another way, parents and their children have little choice in the natural course of things but to love one another. If so, sooner or later the question arises: how do parents determine whether their children really love them if, on the one hand, because of their dependence, they can scarcely afford not to and if, on the other, the traditional signs of adult love--reciprocity, empathic attunement to their heartfelt desires, capacity and willingness to nurture when nurturance is required--are radically lacking?

A common answer that parents have unconsciously resorted to is to look for obedience, compliance, gratitude and respect for everything they have sacrificed for the well-being of their offspring, as substitutive proofs of love. It follows that parents often put undue pressure on their children to show obedience and respect as compensation for their unfulfilled need for reciprocal love. Overlooked is that although children are not equipped to grasp their parents' sense of deprivation, they understand quite well their resentment. What they see clearly, as already mentioned, is that in times of unusual stress, specifically when there is a conflict of interests, when children want or need to do one thing and their parents want or need them to do something else, when customarily discipline is used to resolve unnegotiable issues--the discipline more often than not is applied in a <u>plainly unempathic fashion</u>. And despite classic parental protests that this is for your own good ("One day you'll thank me"), children recognize the disciplinary tactics employed by their parents in times of familial stress are patently self-serving. Intuitively they realize that real love by contrast would have been manifested by signs of empathy and nurturance for the considerable pain entailed through being commanded not to do what they think they really need to do.

Needless to say, this is just what parents characteristically cannot do. Burdened by the sense they are locked into a one-way relationship from which they cannot extricate themselves without serious legal and social repercussions--compare this with even the profoundest adult intimacy where, short of marital legal obligations, you are free to pick up and go at any time--and battling a continual undercurrent of resentment for how much they have to give and how little they get in return, it is almost impossible for them not to feel in moments of family turbulence (i.e., when it seems obvious that their children are acting in unhealthy self-destructive or disrespectful ways) that the least the children can do is to quickly accede to their authority and comply with their commands.

The belief and unconscious demand on their children's part that it is just at these moments that their parents, if they really loved them, would be even more empathically nurturing, is exceedingly hard for grownups to swallow. The upshot, of course, is that when parents, especially under duress, endeavor to mold their children's behavior--that is, to establish rules of being, expectations and standards of conduct to be reinforced if necessary by specified disciplinary sanctions--the modus operandi, more often than not, is to bully their children while simultaneously denying they are doing so.

It follows that the superego which is the heir to all these prohibitions, behavioral modifications and imposed standards of conduct will at least partially reflect, especially in its internalized harshness, the often punitive, self-serving climate from which it originated. It is one ironic measure of the success of such an internalization that adults accede to the demands of their superegos perhaps even more than children do to their actual parents: as though they no longer see, as they once did as children, the underlying narcissism that shaped their ego ideals and the punitive coerciveness that helped forge their conscience. They are not as critical as adults of their superegos as they once were of their actual parents. Another way of saying this is that in the case of the superego, internalization is equivalent to identification with the aggressor. And because their superego, after all, is their's, something they identify with and have some control over, they tend to underestimate the considerable harm--the extent to which they will attack with impunity the best interests of the true self--that can be caused by toxic parental introjects.

THE DYNAMICS OF HUMILIATION

Expressing outright contempt or threatening someone is also, of course, to humiliate them. From the standpoint of asserting transactional dominance, humiliation works because few things are as effective when it comes to demoralizing the other. This is because being humiliated can mean:

1. The person has sunk to a new low in a public way and inexcusably fallen beneath a minimal acceptable level of honorable personal and social conduct. Humiliation implies that parts of the self deemed most shameful and unworthy of exposure, have been exposed. The person therefore feels doubly humiliated--that unsavory behavior or aspects of the self have been unambiguously revealed-- and that he has obviously lacked the dignity necessary to keep it secret.

2. That there is typically at least a temporary traumatic anxiety that one will never be able to restore one's credibility and regain whatever respect the other held for the person just prior to the act of humiliation. The demoralization in part therefore stems from the sense that one has possibly suffered an irreparable loss of prestige in the eyes of the other, not to speak of oneself. Furthermore, one fears that even if the shameful act may eventually be put into a mitigating perspective, it will probably never be completely forgotten (the psychic analogue to having a known criminal record). Also, it can be used as potential ammunition in a future confrontation; certainly the individual who observed or actively triggered it is not likely to forget what occurred. Finally, the painful awareness that whatever doubts

the other has entertained regarding their worth will now be greatly reinforced by the spectacle of their humiliation contributes to their fear that they have just given all their enemies, real or imagined, a club with which to beat them.

3. The person feels unbearably and shamefully out of control. It is humiliating, not only that one can be humiliated, but that one can feel humiliated. As Harry Stack Sullivan (1973) once noted, the real aim of the individual who actively seeks to debase the other, is that the other feel debased. Thus the bully has not really triumphed until the victim acknowledges he has been bullied (typified in the classic kid taunt, "Do you give?") It follows it is shameful to feel humiliated because it seems to indicate an abnormal lack of self esteem; we thereby admit something--that we are at least temporarily degraded--that we almost never admit with a comparable intensity in any other state of mind. It appears tantamount to confessing, "I am a pervert" . . . "I am a criminal" . . . "I am a piece of garbage". Even more incriminating than the internal admission is the emotional identification with and the plain fact (at least for the present) that the person is living out the role of abject victim (taken as an irrefutable unconscious confession of weakness).

It is obvious for all of these reasons that it is terrifying to be humiliated. Part of the panic is that is suddenly appears there may be no clear, safe limit to the extent that one can be debased. There is a dread that if this can happen anything can happen. It is as though the unthinkable has come to pass: like, for example, imagining yourself becoming an actual beggar. Compounding this is that certain acts tend to be self-defining and need only occur once--such as the act of being a coward, a traitor, a criminal, a pervert, or someone who has been humiliated. The person then feels, inasmuch as what happened cannot really be undone, that he or she has in effect been psychically branded.

The other side of the coin is the recognition that if it is true the person does not seem to have a limit when it comes to being debased, it is simultaneously true there is nothing to stop the other from debasing them to their heart's content. For if there is no limit to their impotence when it comes to defending their dignity, there is also no limit to another's potential for exploiting, if they wish, their vulnerability. Which brings us to the dynamics of the one who humiliates.

HOW TO HUMILIATE THE OTHER

1. We have mentioned two favorite ways: to express flat-out contempt and to threaten, coerce and bully. What they share in common is that they both manifest, at least during the act of humiliating the other, a profound perhaps temporarily pathological, absence of empathy. They also represent one of the two principal means of being inhuman: to be heartlessly and aggressively cruel. The second way is to be heartlessly indifferent. Each, of course, contains elements of the other: it is as impossible to be heartlessly cruel without also being unnaturally indifferent to the other's pain as it is to be heartlessly indifferent without also being especially

comfortable (that is, aggressively cruel) vis-à-vis the considerable hurt that such rejection is bound to inflict.

More than anything else, it is this brazen show of seemingly inhuman disregard for the needs of the other's true self that is initially so stunning. The humiliator does not disrespect so much as attack the other's self esteem. To the recipient the assault can feel so intrusive as to constitute a rape of the true self. Not surprisingly, once you have been decisively humiliated, it is hard to feel that the sanctity of the self can ever really be safe.

2. Typically, there is complete denial on the part of the humiliator--unless one is a psychopathic sadist (such as a professional enforcer)--that he is doing what he is doing. The basic form the denial takes is to hide behind the structure and role aspects of power, e.g., the person is only doing his job, candidly pointing out areas that need improvement and telling you what you need to know for your good (unconsciously equated with the bullying parent).

3. After the insult is delivered and denied, the subject is usually quickly changed. Premature closure is rigidly imposed, the unconscious intent and effect being to projectively isolate the trauma solely in the other. This reinforces the recipient's sense of being a pariah, someone cut off from the regard and good opinion of mainstream society: the message being that because they are a pariah they do not merit the privilege of the time that is necessary in which to recover and properly defend themselves. It is thus no small part of the humiliator's power that he can function as a destroyer of other people's reputations.

4. No apology is offered and no need for reparation is manifested. To the victim it is staggering that not only is this person indifferent to his or her narcissistic injury, but feels entitled to inflict it. Not surprisingly paranoia quickly sets in. Either the victim has done something truly monstrous and deserves such abuse or does not--which means that the person administering it is being monstrous. The disturbing question--who is the monster here?--therefore begins to intrude itself. Either way, there is an eerie sense, given the fact that the person who has just humiliated you is acting as though nothing of interpersonal moment has occurred, that you have entered a realm where unnatural events are taking place.

And finally, adding insult to injury, the humiliator shows no surprise at what has happened, no recognition that a significant upheaval, a crisis of confidence has just been precipitated in the victim. Aside from indifference so extreme as to be toxic, the fact such an attitude shows an obvious expectation of the other's debasement is in itself demoralizing.

What follows, in order to make this clearer, are some brief examples, snapshots of power plays (to be developed in greater detail in the following chapter) that are based on some of the dynamics that have so far been depicted.

BEATING SOMEONE TO THE PUNCH

1. Here the unconscious intention is to disarm the other's power to belittle you by launching a preemptive strike, but against yourself.

2. By acting as though one is aware of a consistent flaw of character or a dysfunctional pattern of behavior one hopes, again unconsciously, to eliminate the need in the other to comment on something obviously true but which the person may not or has not yet given signs of being aware. (I am reminded of a patient, a woman with a history of sabotaging her relationships with men who, upon becoming anxious on a first date with a man she found exceptionally attractive, out of the blue, blurted, "I know my problem is to drive a man away and then put the blame on him. I don't want to do that with you.")

3. The most common result is that the would-be criticizer is hard put to articulate or paraphrase the self-criticisms which have just been revealed without seeming suspiciously redundant and perhaps possessed of an inner need to put down the person.

4. In addition, there is a sense one is being refreshingly honest in acknowledging a supposedly cardinal flaw (an instance of what I once called narcissistic honesty: the attempt to ward off expected criticism for an unconsciously perceived failing by brazenly admitting it as though to thereby indicate that, far from being ashamed, one is actually proud of what one has often been accused of; thus, as can be often noted, someone who is known to be hostile and insensitive will defend himself by volunteering, "Yes, I am blunt."). It follows that the preemptive introjection of a potentially toxic criticism--a version perhaps of what Christopher Bollas calls 'extractive introjection', 1987--can be deceptively reassuring: what before was perceived as a psychic field of unknown negative capability has become just another internal voice--to be modulated, contradicted, laughed at, transformed, disguised and so on. Above all, the critical voice is now one's own. It is empowering and a popular fantasy to be in charge of how one's major weaknesses are to be framed; when they are to be dealt with and when put on the shelf. And, of course, as one's own chief critic one has, if one wishes to and knows how, at least a chance of being endlessly empathic with one's worst shortcomings.

"I'VE GOTTA BE ME"

Variations of this are, "I need my space" and the more aggressive "You're suffocating me". The implication is that the overriding issue is freedom and autonomy versus suppression. Thus, at bottom, the conflict is political rather than purely personal, and because it is political it transcends the pettiness of ordinary interpersonal transactions. No longer does the issue revolve around the individual's frustrations, insufficient gratifications, communicational and relational impasses--the issue is nothing less than the civil rights of the self.

There are few more effective measures for immobilizing the other in an interpersonal fray than to politicize what is clearly not political. To do so is to introduce power into a relationship where it is not needed. The question therefore becomes--what does this accomplish?

1. Perhaps foremost is that it almost immediately freezes the dynamics of intersubjective relating. Empathy, growth, reciprocal exploration become irrelevant as one retrospectively scrutinizes the recent history of the relationship to see if there have really been infringements of the other's rights, as claimed.

2. On one level, the message seems to be that morality, conscience and one's ego ideal (the way things should be) have just entered the picture with a bang. From a psychodynamic point of view, the person politicizing the relationship is acting as though she has assumed the high moral ground. In actuality, pure power--once it has detached itself from being in the service of the deepest relational needs of the true self, which includes both the needs and rights of the other as well--tends to operate on a rather low level of narcissistic greed. Under the smokescreen of moralistic political posturing, it typically aims to ravenously feed its neediness.

3. Because of what one might call the bad faith (Sartre, 1956) of such a power play (unconsciously the person senses the lack of any real psychic significance) there is often an attempt to end it quickly by winning. From this standpoint, winning may not psychologically represent a need to triumph as much as a need to terminate a dirty deal and rapidly wash one's hands of it.

4. Finally, it is the mystifying ability of a power play such as politicizing a relationship to render all other relational matters as seemingly trivial, that makes it so potent as a strategy of interpersonal control.

"I GET SO ANGRY WITH YOU BECAUSE I LOVE AND TRUST YOU SO MUCH."

This effectively disarms the other by taking the sting out of his or her narcissistic injury, by reframing it as the produce of love and not disrespect. The inference is that what appears to be frank abuse is the byproduct of being so close to someone that you fee free to unload all your feelings, negative as well as positive. This, of course, puts subtle pressure on the other to reciprocate by trusting that when the person seems abusive, he or she is only letting their true emotions come out in a way that is consistent with a loving, although real (and therefore flawed) person. Thus behavior that can be blatantly hostile, distancing or dismissive can be plausibly set within the context of an admirably honest and open relationship. What is significant, and typically overlooked, is that now absolutely nothing needs to be done vis-à-vis working on the underlying issues and impediments to intimacy: whatever was in the other that may have been unconsciously triggering the outpouring of anger or in the offender who perhaps was only waiting to be provoked, has been upstaged by the grandeur of the pseudo reparative gesture.

THE FIGHT FOR MEANING

It is commonplace and often noted that people-- especially when engaged in conversation--tend to be defensive about their interpretation of what is meaningful and what is not. This is particularly clear in the case of geniuses in various disciplines, that is with those rare individuals who have invested an abnormal amount of psychic energy in the consolidation of a profoundly specialized point of view on an aspect of the world they find uniquely meaningful. (John Horgan, 1996, who interviewed many such geniuses in his wonderfully stimulating The End of Science observed that they much preferred to prepare whatever they said, and rarely seemed to be actually thinking while speaking.) To deny, outright attack, sabotage, minimize or devalue this meaningfulness can then be tantamount to an assault on the core of their being. Hence, the notorious and venomous intellectual wars that can be seen to flourish on subjects that to the rest of us seem almost pointlessly abstract.

It follows with ordinary people, who do not usually expend prodigious energy in fortifying a preferred perspective, whatever interpersonal meaning they elect to endorse and defend will accordingly be considerably less rooted in objective reality, and much more subjectively colored. The meanings most dear to them will most likely be idiosyncratic ones, culled from their personal life histories. From a transactional standpoint, the greatest meaning will perhaps be attributed to how each regards the other and how the other is perceived to regard the self.

But it is extremely difficult, if not impossible, to articulate, let alone persuasively frame such interpersonal meanings in the short shelf life of a dynamically changing interaction. It may be because of this few people try, especially when engaged in casual socializing, and conversations tend to be unconscious collusions designed to boycott the recognition of personal significance. Toward that end social customs regulating acceptable conversational fare (such as weather talk) have evolved to get us, with a semblance of dignity, safely through transactions that, more often than not, are relatively meaningless.

In spite of this, meaning invariably seeps through. No matter how great the mutual pretense is that only interpersonal pleasantries are being bandied about, that nothing threatening is underfoot, that no mean-spirited devaluation is in the offing, it is almost inconceivable that something about how each really feels about the other will not at least be subliminally communicated and received. Regardless of how strenuously each party strives to suppress what is personally meaningful, at least the shadow of the true self will fall upon the transaction. And there will be hints of how much deference, genuine interest and possible validation as opposed to equally authentic boredom, disinterest or frank, if masked, contempt is implicit in the interaction. Such hints can be manifold. How much energy is required to uphold the facade of civility, how many defensive operations are necessary to get one through the encounter, the degree of tension that is elicited, how open, warm and playfully friendly one is capable of being--will all point to the real underlying object relation.

It follows that the unconscious registration of these hints--although it may fall far short of producing those polysemous instances which Freud termed psychical intensities--cannot help but lend an air of some significance to what has transpired. More often than not, unless the relationship is an especially intimate one, such significance will be quickly aborted: incipient interpersonal meaning, like incipient interpersonal intimacy, is exceedingly easy to nip in the bud. And because it is the path of least resistance--as opposed to the considerably more risky venture of endeavoring to mutually spontaneously elaborate whatever seems individually meaningful--not surprisingly that is what usually happens.

But what about the latent meaning that, in spite of transactional restraints, manages to escape and make its fleeting presence felt, if only unconsciously? Sensing that psychic space in the other for the reception and nurturing of such meaning cannot or will not be allowed, there is an almost instinctive anxiety concerning the fate of unprocessed emanations from the true self. As a result meaning tends to get <u>defended</u>, instead of elaborated. And the tactics of power now enter the picture. What gets articulated is not what the person says or means, thinks or feels, but position papers of the self, shared conventional beliefs and ideas guaranteed to win polite approval.

Power is used when--as opposed to developing hints of meaning--there is a concerted attempt to manipulate pseudo-meaning in order to influence the other's behavior (the classic example being perhaps the trial attorney in the American criminal justice system). What often follows is an acknowledged unconscious fight for meaning: the person tries to control what is to be accepted as the meaning of the interaction by aggressively trying to orchestrate its onset, flow, duration and termination. There may be no better example of this than the seemingly benign inquiry, "Do you understand?" which, beneath its pose of facilitating communication, contains a number of hidden power assumptions: that the interrogator is the one who is capable of knowing when meaning has been reached, when there is no point in continuing, when what is important is to ascertain if the auditor has been able to adequately keep pace with, receive and digest the significance of what has just been presented. A crucial corollary of this, of course, is that the auditor is not on the same meaning level as the interrogator, needs tutoring, and cannot autonomously clarify for himself when he knows something and when he does not. The irony of such a fight (at bottom the struggle over whose interpretation of the encounter will prevail) is that meaning--by not being allowed to evolve, be felt or experienced--soon becomes meaningless.

TOUGH LOVE

Monica is an attractive young actress who complains of being unable to find a man who is willing to make a commitment to her. She blames this on her father, a philandering airline pilot who conducted affairs with a number of women in various cities, was eventually discovered to be an actual bigamist and who abandoned his traumatized family for good when Monica was eleven years old. In the session, she is recounting an exchange between herself and her girlfriend occurring in the kitchen of her apartment just after she has sobbingly told the sad story of how her latest boyfriend--someone to whom she has devoted the past three years of her life--but who, nevertheless, has seen fit to emphatically decline her desperate ultimatum that they finally move in together. Expecting nothing less than total sympathy and support, Monica is taken aback, and subsequently enraged, when her boyfriend suddenly seizes her by the shoulders, vigorously shakes her and angrily exhorts her to, above all, "Be strong!".

When I try to ask Monica what it is about her girlfriend's admittedly heavy-handed rescue operation that so upset her, she simply says, "I felt weak". That was as good a definition (Monica had hit the nail on the head), I later realized, as there is of how people often feel when they are treated to what is referred to as tough love. They find it almost impossible to feel good about themselves. For the natural reaction is to suspect that the other thinks they are behaving in a dangerously, shamefully or self-indulgently weak fashion--what else could explain the manifest alarm in their minds?

Yet, since the other is acting as a self-appointed advocate on one's behalf, it indicates she at least believes the person is in legitimate trouble or why bother to invest her energy? While this apparently sincere concern, expressed through an urgent call to marshall one's strength, is appreciated on a certain level, it is quite demoralizing on another: the person rightly feels that it is their responsibility to take care of themselves, but the fact that the other finds it necessary to preempt it strongly suggests that their public persona of being self-sufficient is less than convincing. There seems to be an obvious mixed message here: on the one hand, the other values the person enough to volunteer to sponsor their survival, and believes in their potential resources enough to grow excited over their prospects for recovery; yet clearly does not trust the person enough to independently work things out on their own or even to be an equal collaborator in determining a promising strategy for overcoming the predicament at hand. It is telling that the counsel of the one in trouble is not sought and often little interest is expressed in discussing the life-saving, precious tough love advice that is being eagerly dispensed. The assumption, seemingly, is that the person who appears lost in their destructive ways will wake up and 'get it'. It follows, for all of these reasons, that tough love, even when well-intended--and often it is not--is infantalizing.

From a psychodynamic point of view, tough love--when it is not being employed in a social service setting as a trendy new technique for curbing wayward youngsters--that is, when it is being unconsciously acted out between consenting adults, cannot help but raise some profound questions. Perhaps foremost is--how tough on the other in the service love can one be? And when is one being too tough?

This is a much harder question when it is applied to consenting adults than when it is applied to parents and their children or to people and their idea of God. The issue of how much pain and affliction can be permitted or imposed on human beings in the name of love is handled by religions primarily by reference to faith and the redemptive value of suffering. That is, no matter how awesome, widespread and repetitious the cruelty and torture that so-called acts of God--disease, natural catastrophes, the disturbing fact not only of the presence of evil, but that unspeakably evil deeds are allowed to be perpetrated upon good people without divine intervention--visit upon us, the believer must trust that ultimately God's designs are infinitely merciful, loving and just.

Through such exhortation, the seemingly unbearable and meaningless pain that is an inextricable part of the fabric of human existence is explained away as being but an earthly mirage, the product of our very finite understanding: mysterious are the ways of God. What this means, of course, is that unbounded human suffering can be acceptable, provided that we are totally not responsible for it. How great is our need to be exonerated from any charge that we are wilfully inflicting unnecessary suffering on another can be seen from the fact that 'to play God' is considered perhaps the ultimate of moral iniquities. (This may become clearer if we conduct the following thought experiment: imagine a person, a doctor who is a religious fanatic, who is discovered to have purposely inoculated a series of innocent patients with the virus of a serious disease, and who sincerely asserts he was doing it in the name of love--to give them access to the benefits of redemptive suffering. Let us further imagine that, uncannily, all of the patients subsequently testify that the eventual gain in wisdom and insight as a result of having and overcoming the disease more than compensated for what first seemed senseless and terrifying suffering. Yet even with this fantastically improbable best-case scenario, it is hardly possible such a person would not be universally decreed a moral monster or lunatic.)

The crucial point, of course, is that the imposition of suffering upon others cannot be fobbed off on God when it comes to being intimate with people we care about. Only we are responsible for the pain that we inflict in the name of love. Only we must recognize there is no such thing as an act or expression of love that does not also entail a compromise between the amount of nurturance that is given and the amount that is withheld. And since every act, no matter how well-intentioned and how much we desire to nourish the entire self of the other, has intrinsic limits, we are always forced to decide, consciously or unconsciously, what aspects of the other we are going to exclude. Indeed, almost from the beginning of life it becomes obvious that there cannot be perfect symbiosis between parent and child, and that the illusion of necessary infantile omnipotence--regardless of how well managed by the famous Winnicottian good enough mother (1965)--must soon yield to a separation, individuation and conflict of interests. As Freud noted, no human mother can fail to fall far short of meeting her infant/child's needs many times: a series of disappointments over time that consolidate into a residue of hate. If the person, then, that gave life and most nourished us can periodically, consciously or unconsciously, provoke hatred, how much more so can the stranger whom one meets as an adult and falls in love with? It follows each of us must recognize that there is an undercurrent of ambivalence, a mixture of love and hate in even the best of relationships. Even and although we may desperately not want to--we know we must often disappoint, frustrate, alienate and anger our love object. And, of course, due to the inevitable incompatibility of interests between lovers, the ordinary narcissistic investment in solitary desires and the occasional need to aggressively express psychic elements of hate, there will be times when we have no wish to satisfy the other. In other words, there will be circumstances when we decide it is in our best interests to refuse to satisfy the needs of the person we love, realizing full well that the consequences most likely will be at least some pain and suffering incurred by the other.

The question then becomes--in the name of autonomy-- how much pain and suffering are we permitted to indirectly cause the other to whom we are involved in a committed intimate relationship, while we pursue the fulfillment of our legitimate individual needs? At what point does autonomous self-actualization become indifference, narcissism or even subtle torture of the love object? And if we choose to go in the opposite direction--sacrificing our autonomy for the self-actualization of the other--at what point does our self-denial become, not love, but masochism?

By contrast, for parents the issue of reciprocal autonomy vis-à-vis their relationship to their children can seem deceptively clearcut. As designated guardians of their children's present and future psychical and physical well being, they can remind themselves they have extensive privileges, sanctioned by society and the law, to restrain their behavior and administer discipline when necessary, within reason, whenever they see fit. Although they cannot overtly or recognizably abuse their children, they can effectively reject them, withhold approval, barely listen to them, condescendingly talk down to them, ridicule them for their failures, order them about, bully them, often conduct themselves in a mean-spirited way and (supposedly constructively) criticize them to their heart's content. All of which, of course, can then be rationalized as being 'for their own good'. Someone, therefore, can bring up their children--meeting all of the official criteria of society and the law for being a proper parent--without ever really enjoying their company, respecting them as individuals or even loving them for their own sake.

What this means is that parents, so long as they do not transgress any of the existing (and rapidly growing) laws against child abuse, enjoy considerable leverage when it comes to depriving, frustrating and making their children plain miserable, all in the name of education, nurturance and discipline. Sadly, the fact that they have access to incomparably more life experience, that they are assumed, until proven otherwise, to be operating under a biological, social and moral imperative to love their children is used to justify the innumerable lapses of good judgment, the failures to act compassionately and decently and the almost universal tendency of parents to scapegoat their children for their strictly private suffering.

There is a sense in which the standard to which parents adhere for depriving their children of their freedom and forcing them to do what they don't want to do is analogous to the one used by the American Psychiatric Association for depriving adults of their customary constitutional right to live their lives autonomously: if their behavior should pose a manifest danger to themselves or others. And presumably children, until they reach the age at which they are legally entitled to move out on their own and lead independent lives if they choose, do not really know nearly as well as their parents when their behavior poses such a manifest danger to themselves or others. Finally, in both cases it is assumed that the pain and suffering caused by depriving someone--whether as wayward child or mentally disabled adult--of their personal freedom will be more than compensated for by avoidance of even greater pain and suffering to which their actions were surely leading them.

What is overlooked in all of this is how such a system of belief, indoctrination, coercion and rationalization is supposed to engender--almost miraculously it seems at the precise time the individual achieves the age at which freedom from parental prohibition is legally guaranteed--the ability to live life autonomously. The conventional, societal and educational answer is that a foundation for healthy, autonomous functioning will have been laid by the parental setting of proper limits, by serving early on in the home as a future role model and by rewarding and reinforcing independent behavior as it occurs that is deemed phase-appropriate (the first time, for example, one ties one's shoelaces, brushes one's teeth, crosses the street alone, goes to school, learns to swim, washes the dishes, goes to camp, drives a car, has a date and so on).

All of which sounds fine on paper. In practice, however, as mentioned, and especially when there is a conflict between what parents want and what their children want, the modus operandi for restraining or correctively disciplining children will be, in one measure or another, to bully them. What this comes down to is that while children may at least in theory have equal rights with their parents in terms of not being abused, greater rights than their parents in regard to being financially supported, fed, clothed, raised, cared for and educated--their right to conduct their lives autonomously is vastly inferior to that of their parents. Since children, of course, much of the time, at least prior to the onset of rebellious adolescent drives, do not want to lead autonomous lives, the power that parents have, reinforced as it is by their children's collusive dependence, is both enormous and irresistibly easy to abuse.

The fact such power is so often abused does not mean that parents necessarily aim to take unfair advantage of their children. Much more likely is it that they would like to use this power fairly, but find that is by no means as simple as it sounds. Think of the classic difficulty parents face when challenged by their children to explain and justify the rationale behind their mandates. There are reasons for this. To honestly try to exercise power fairly entails, especially when there is a gross inequity, the attempt initially to level the playing field. But to do that requires in turn relinquishing some of one's power, so as to more equitably redistribute it which, again, cannot be done without seriously empathizing with the position of the weaker party. It immediately becomes clear that a principal motivation for using power unfairly is that one is unwilling or unable to do the work necessary to exercise it fairly. This, of course, is even more glaringly apparent in adult employer-employee relationships on those infrequent occasions when a superior is questioned as to the fairness of a specific policy or company decision. This is typically met first with a recitation of the party line which, if not duly swallowed, is followed up with the standard, "This is the way we do things around here."

Ironically, for all of these reasons, it is <u>more efficient to exercise power than to explicate, negotiate or redistribute it</u>. Nowhere is this more evident than in the power disequilibrium that exists in the traditional nuclear family between parents and their offspring. After all, if parents really had to continuously negotiate and reason with their children instead of instructing, ordering and disciplining them, one can only wonder how many necessary childhood tasks would ever get done. Nevertheless, in spite of its pragmatic utility, the inequity of the distribution of power in the nuclear family can only be a poor training ground for future requirements as an adult to interpersonally deal with a conflict of interests--especially in an intimate love relationship--where the right and need to live autonomously is presumably equal and therefore cannot be simply handled by one person taking complete charge.

It follows no small part of the struggle and work that goes into the maintenance of a genuinely intimate relationship is the energy required to walk the tightrope between living autonomously (respecting and loving one's own best interests in a healthy way) and empathically resonating with and nurturing the true self of the other. Although they are supposed to be complementary, in real life they do not seem to go well together.

In families, such issues have tended to be settled in an either/or fashion. An aftermath of this is that often as grownups the tactics of tough love--as an euphemistic way to smuggle in power as a means of resolving unnegotiable differences of being--will seem an appealing strategy for avoiding the serious reciprocal demands of intimacy.

INTIMATE GIVING

So far the uses of power that have been described here have been abuses. To give, by contrast, an idea of what the fair use of power in, for example, an intimate relationship might be, it would help to clarify, first, what I mean by intimate giving.

An act of intimate giving--by definition the antithesis of a power operation--begins with a clear focusing on the other's needs which entails an empathic reading of the underlying dynamics, which are often exceedingly complex, of the specific request. To have reached this position, however--the interpersonal vantage point from which someone can meaningfully and realistically be nurturing in even a seemingly trivial way to another person--it is necessary that one will have managed, at least temporarily, to have set aside normal but interfering needs so as to be able to invest the required energy. Since the investment of energy can often be considerable, the individual must be prepared to spend a sufficient amount of time, and it is therefore a general characteristic of an act of intimate giving that before it is initiated there will be a decision that, somehow, the appropriate time will be found. It is important to realize, however, that this conception of time is not measured, as time traditionally is, in standardized segments, but in terms of being available for as long as it takes to respond in a nurturing way: i.e., the clock it goes by is developmental.

Because an act of intimate giving therefore begins typically with a clear and in-depth perception of what is behind what the other seems to be asking for, it is almost always empathic in nature. It is never purely informational even when the other seems to be seeking nothing more consequential than, let us say, the correct time of day and the reason for this is that it is primarily concerned with the interpersonal context out of which the question emerges. So, for example, if the person requesting time is really expressing a sense of being somewhat discouraged with the way his or her personal time is progressing, the other might--after supplying the desired information--also communicate, non-verbally, that there is an awareness that more is needed than just information. Put another way, it is a mark of intimate giving that it sizes up and takes into account, consciously or unconsciously, the relational and developmental possibilities that are present. In so doing, it transcends the immediate here and now need and anticipates the future.

In addition, intimate giving is:

Congruent. There is a matching of what is truly needed with what is really being given.

Nurturing. Although it is characteristically taken for granted in any posture of giving--that what is being offered is, of course, going to be helpful or at the very least is intended to be helpful--it is surprisingly rare when help that is given is even minimally nurturing. Real nurturing implies help that is more than patchwork--that is developmental inasmuch as it is capable of facilitating, via a timely and benign relationship, a person's progress in a healthy direction. Because of this, intimate giving is more often tilted towards the developmental future (best long range interest of the individual) as opposed to the immediate assuagement of transient difficulties. It is therefore nurturing, and is perceived that way, in a sense that legitimate but superficial helpfulness can never be. I believe this is borne out by the fact--when you think about it--of how infrequent it is that someone will have the experience of being really grateful for the right help being given at the right time.

Meaningful. Because an act of intimate giving generally strives to reach some part of the core of the other's psyche, it cannot be the meaningless experience that is characteristic of transactions based on power.

Reciprocal. It is a sign of an act of intimacy that it aspires to make contact with, resonate with, and to be known by as well as to know the other. From an interactive standpoint, therefore, it typically tends toward reciprocity. It is a tendency reinforced by an absence of a power orientation, which traditionally has depended on the advantages conferred by hierarchical and unilateral distancing. The result is an intimate transaction whose center of gravity, more likely than not, will be the same for both parties.

Revelatory. When someone is deeply attuned to what the other wants--in spite of the fact attention and energy seems directed away from the self--there is an inevitable and significant disclosure of who one is. By its nature intimacy entails a relaxation and readjustment of one's boundaries, that is a prelude to the expansion of and flowing out of the self that is part of its process. To the degree that an act of intimacy entails such an expressive movement of the true self, it will tend to reveal what otherwise would be hidden or at least clouded by normal defensive operations.

Serious. Transactions based on power employ a host of strategies designed to trivialize, diminish, shrink and reduce the other as a means of relieving the internalized pressure people feel to constantly interpersonally relate. By contrast, an intimate interaction is characterized by its intuitive grasp of what is most existentially pressing to the other. Accordingly it cannot help but take the situation of the other seriously, respect it, and therefore use language, as expeditiously as possible, to express issues of the self, and not--as is common in power operations--to erect a diverting non-communicative facade of desensitizing superficiality.

Forthcoming. An intimate act is one in which a person elects to reduce the psychical distance between self and other in order to be in close enough range to make greater contact if desired, as well as to be taken in more fully by another who is so inclined. The result is that the receiver of intimate giving often has the novel experience of another self which is approaching or forthcoming but neither in an intrusive nor aggressive fashion.

Binding. Even a fleeting intimacy can have the effect of inaugurating a bond between two people--who previously otherwise were not connected--which can later be built upon. In this sense, intimacy is really a foundational glue that binds people together and is probably the best predictor of longevity in human relations. As an authentic bridge between psyches it is resistant to normal interpersonal wear and tear and it does not tend, upon the first frontal attack, to crumble like a house of cards.

Trusting. Underlying the use of power operations there is often the paranoid fear of being exposed--which in its extreme form leads to the interpersonal philosophy that offense is the best defense, with its concomitant strategy of the preemptive attack. By contrast, trust is at the center, or at the very least at the beginning, of any interaction that can be designated as intimate. If one thinks about it, to enter into a relationship with another that is in any way congruent, nurturing, meaningful, reciprocal, revelatory (or possesses any of the traits thus far mentioned) is also to take a risk. In most cases, the risk is not to one's flesh and bone but to a part of the self that has become unavoidably denuded through the act of being intimate. Inasmuch as there is danger, courage is required, and it is no small part of the reason people generally feel good about themselves after they have attempted to be intimate, that they know, on some level, that they have been uncharacteristically courageous. The trust that is involved, therefore, is that one--by having the courage to take the risk that is involved in being intimate--will not thereby hurt oneself in some unforeseen way. But trust, being a human attribute, is not only variable, but dynamically sensitive to the interpersonal context out of which it arises--which means there is always a chance that it can seriously backfire. When it does, or when one thinks it does, there is the familiar dread that perhaps one has taken too big a risk, exposed oneself unnecessarily and in fact wrongly trusted. In its extreme form, such fears are indistinguishable from paranoia--the traumatic perception that far from strengthening oneself through a heightened and nurturing mutuality, one has actually laid oneself bare to an untrustworthy other. So, although trust, as I believe, is an indispensable constitute of an intimate act, there is a sense in which it is never far removed from and is linked to (if only as a negative potentiality) its inverse, paranoia.

Profoundly personal. Implicit in many transactions based on power is the grandiose belief that efficient and productive impersonality can be a suitable and sometimes complete substitute for the fundamental need of the self to be confirmed in any interpersonal encounter, no matter how fleeting; and that by offering the benefits to be plausibly derived from an impersonal, professional or business relationship you have thereby delivered something of such value that the need to relate in a genuinely human way can be justifiably relinquished. In sharp contrast to this, an instance of intimate giving, whatever else it may be, is always, on some level, profoundly personal. While it may also be realistic or objective, it is never abstract, dry or simply logical. It is not politicized. Regardless of the belief system that is held, there is the sense that the person is relating according to some distinctive inner logic that in turn is in harmony with the true self.

These are just some of the key traits that characterize intimate giving. It is obvious that intimate giving does not rely upon the tactics of power; does not attempt to gain deference through intimidation. It pursues, instead, from the other the respect that is freely given in response to an experience of being nurtured. It does not reduce complicated emotional requests, which may involve multi-determined, dynamic and often unconscious forces, to the status of pedestrian one-dimensional questions.

Intimate giving does not entail sleight of hand. It is not subversive, bullying, or pseudo-logical. It is not an agent of the false self. It does not attempt to appear giving by courageously revealing a shameful trauma from the past. By contrast, the intimate disclosure that is a fundamental component of ongoing intimacy far transcends the simple, howsoever dramatic telling of painful, horrible secrets.

An act of intimate giving, as opposed to a transaction based on power, is a process rather than a one-time, cathartic experience. It is not a confession. It is not looking for release from pent-up childhood traumas. It is not the expression, or cultivation, of a "victim" identity. It is not melodramatically larger than life, sensationalistic or titillating.

When conflict is involved it typically will hinge on the capacity, on the one hand for reciprocal nurturing and, on the other, on the attendant anxieties concerning incorporation, transgression or dissolution of one's boundaries, and the paranoid fear of the dangers ensuing from too much closeness. What is more, such conflicts as do exist will be contained rather than acted out.

Finally, sensation will not be overvalued and pursued for its own sake. Relationships will not be viewed primarily as a means for the achievement of exciting experiences. Instead they will be appraised--not from the standpoint of whether one is getting or is likely to get what one wants--but for their power to nurture. The philosophy of Machiavellianism, so preferred by power players, will not be substituted for the practice of honestly negotiating and endeavoring to work through substantive relational differences. While satisfactions are, of course, sought, their attainment tends to be deferred and the pleasures they bring are more likely to be the aftermath rather than the immediate aim of the interaction. This is because there will be what Bion (1992) has referred to as the capacity to tolerate frustration, normal depression and the pain intrinsic to emotional development.

An intimate transaction, therefore, is never the product of a hunger for overstimulation, suspense or immediate gratification, the kind of hunger which is regularly fed by televised daytime soap opera. Instead, it finds its gratifications typically in a meaningful discovery, developmental unfolding and a cohesive sense of process.

Yet, if it is true that it is the element of intimacy in a human relationship that ultimately most deeply satisfies, why is it that it is so rarely achieved? The answer, I believe, is that it is far easier to become involved in a relationship that promises short-term gratifications and predictable, swiftly attainable pleasures than to try to cope with and to pursue the elusive, generally delayed, far more risky-- but for that reason incomparably more profound, satisfying and even entertaining--rewards intrinsic to the type of human bonding characterized by intimacy.

The great psychoanalyst, D.W. Winnicott, once said that "moral education is no substitute for love". To which you can add that the technique of intimacy--the covert aim to use power to manipulate closeness--whether as practiced by the mental health profession or by the individual who is looking for a shortcut, is no substitute for intimacy.

Yet, as I wrote in The Singles Scene (Alper, 1996), "every psychotherapist and student of human nature has seen instances of true intimacy and intimate giving and knows that it exists (otherwise, there would be no point in writing this book). It is important that it occurs, and when it does--even if the final outcome is not a happy one providing the expected gratifications--there are few who do not feel that all the effort and the trouble were well worth it and that the process itself was inherently enriching."

For all of these reasons, it follows that transactions based not on intimacy but on power tend to be short-lived. In our present day culture of narcissism, there are literally thousands of such brief interludes, abortive intimacies, what I call relational snapshots--all products in one way or another of the dynamics that have been depicted--and in the next chapter I explore in greater depth some of the more prevalent examples.

CHAPTER THREE
Snapshots
A HOT FRIEND COOLING

The lament of Shakespeare's Brutus over the waning interest of his erstwhile passionate ally, Cassius, after hundreds of years, still rings in our ears. Today, to a significant extent, the story of relationships is the story of disappointment, burnout and estrangement and the office of the modern psychotherapist is often sought as a kind of psychic recovery room following the traumatic amputation of a prized portion of the self.

Although such loss is most commonly presented from the perspective of the person who feels abandoned, it was Samuel, an unemployed, embittered thirty-five year old actor, who made the case most memorably in therapy for the necessity, and often the intense pleasure to be derived from deserting a relationship gone sour. No small part of this pleasure was the palpable consternation of someone who-- habituated to smugly taking Samuel's friendship for granted--was now clueless as to how to account for the sudden and radical withdrawal of his former interest.

In therapy, Samuel would solemnly detail the method by which he would exorcise from his life the presence of a friend who had hurt him too many times to ever be forgiven again. The first and most important step was involuntary and internal; but which would pave the way for his strategy of deadly withdrawal. He would wake up one morning and begin brooding about a particular friend who had disappointed him, or be walking in the street, and he would experience (as he described it) an epiphany of "nothingness". Where before there had been a complicated network of feelings, both tender and hateful, now there was a void, a numbness.

It was a numbness that was liberating. Shorn of his feelings, especially the feeling of guilt, he was free to express the hostility he had up until now kept hidden. Samuel could at last do what he had really wanted to do for a long time. Should he encounter the friend in question in public he would most likely nod curtly, continue to walk and make a point of not stopping to converse. Out of the corner of his eye he would steal a glance at his friend's face, hoping to catch signs of unmistakable dismay. If thereafter the puzzled friend would telephone (perhaps hoping to clarify what seemed a mystifying rejection), Samuel would screen the message with perverse pleasure and, of course, refuse to return the call.

And that would be just the beginning. What had seemed a troubling, although isolated incident, would soon be repeated. Samuel would make sure of that. He would bide his time, waiting for the secretly blacklisted friend, to make a predictable overture for getting together: to suggest perhaps meeting for a drink, attending an interesting party that was being planned, taking advantage of some complimentary tickets to an off-Broadway show, or arranging for an extended, catch-up conversation. Now there could be no doubt--when once again samuel would inexplicably fail to respond in his customary way--that something was wrong. But what?

Phase two, the 'guessing game', was the part that Samuel most enjoyed, when he would feel like an unseen puppeteer pulling the strings that made the relationship go. From his own periodic bouts of paranoia he well knew just how tantalizing and unsettling the sudden disappearance of a presumed friend could be. He knew how doubts that could not be answered and would not end concerning the motives for abandonment would over time prove unbearable. He knew that few things are as imposing, as unbreakable, as bottomless as silence. To Samuel, silence, deftly timed, could therefore be both eloquent and passionate. The more he would withdraw, the stronger he felt. The less he spoke, the more he was understood. The more absent he became, the more present, unavoidable and terrible his anger would appear. He had only to keep the mystery alive, to lurk in the background, to record the whispers and innuendos surrounding his orchestrated disappearance reported back to him by mutual acquaintances, to note the confusion, the hurt feelings, the loss of face that was being fended off, and the revenge that he thirsted after would surely be his.

Although few would care to go to the Iago lengths of a Samuel, the cooling off of the intensity of any given relationship is a natural and probably universal occurrence. Providing that the loss of interest is roughly reciprocal and that there is some mutual acceptance of what is happening, this usually does not pose an unsurmountable problem. By contrast, few things are as unsettling as the realization that a supposed friend is gradually or suddenly withdrawing a customary level of warmth, interest and friendliness without an appropriate explanation (and who, when challenged, will typically deny what he or she is doing).

The disappearing other will then immediately become more mysterious and, to a certain extent, more desirable. Automatically the person who is feeling rebuffed will take note of the other's growing absence and begin to pay more attention: either silently observing the signs of withdrawal in order to determine their hidden significance or actively courting the former friend in the hope of rekindling the old warmth. Sooner or later, however, it will become apparent that the other is not only acting mysteriously, but, much more to the point, is being mysteriously angry.

The power of mysterious anger to manipulate and control its target is considerable. There is, for example, its aura of the wounded victim, the sufferer too proud to speak who is silently licking his wounds. There is the intrigue engendered by a sense of danger: doubt about the source of the anger can subtly change into doubt over what would be a safe defense--in turn giving rise to an anxiety that an attack could come at any time and that anything could provoke it. The fact that the other is being strangely secretive about his anger can suggest not only that it may be too extreme to be voiced but that the other has lost, or really has so little trust in the person's capacity to understand his point of view or to make reasonable changes, that it is pointless to bring it up. Furthermore, there is the distinct possibility that the anger was so toxic that it completely nullified the store of positive nurturance gathered in the course of the relationship and sufficiently numbed the other so that what is now being manifested is 'genuine' indifference rather than sullen withdrawal.

Whatever the cause may be, the other clearly has undergone a fairly dramatic transformation in his perspective on the value of being in contact with the person. The new relationship is a non-reciprocal and secret one and this cannot fail to tantalize someone who may alternately feel excluded, abandoned, punished, banished, devalued and discarded. It is also tantalizing to withhold any realistic promise of closure to whatever the problem may be. After all, until the individual who is acting so unlike himself says otherwise, there is always a chance that the former relationship may somehow be restored and thus there is a small ray of hope. Typically, of course, this is not the case: the one who is withdrawing intends to do so even more, but rather than invest in the relationship to the extent of being open about it, he would prefer to be mysterious concerning the true status of what is going on (thus being able to strongly influence the person, but with only a minimum of input and interaction). Not surprisingly, in the worst case scenario, the erstwhile friend, yielding to paranoid suspicion, may conclude that a trial of the past relationship has already been secretly conducted by the other and that a sentence has been rendered without the person ever having had the chance to be present.

To terminate in a clandestine fashion and radically withdraw from an ongoing relationship with some history to it is only one extreme measure of being mysterious in a manipulative way. There are other methods. Indeed, it might be said, from the broadest possible interpersonal perspective, that each and every relationship--from the standpoint of warmth, friendliness, openness, depth of feeling, spontaneity and degree of intimacy--has a certain set point, a homeostatic temperature to which it strives to return. (Of course, if the relationship truly grows the set point will correspondingly expand, but until a new plateau has been established it will characteristically tend to be stable.)

Now although each dynamic moment is different and will fluctuate upwards or downwards from the particular set point, the person--unconsciously responding to his own predetermined, interactive temperature as though to a relational thermostat--will typically make efforts to counter the vicissitudes of random mood deviations. Thus, for example, if he is feeling unduly cranky, depressed or withdrawn, he may attempt to balance this by an added show of empathy or thoughtfulness towards the other or, at the very least, an admission of being sub-par (e.g., "I guess I'm having a bad day"). Contrarily, if he is acting uncharacteristically joyful and celebratory because of some expected good fortune, sooner or later--when the elation wears off--he may unconsciously compensate for this by, perhaps, a retrospective show of bemusement over his recent somewhat manic mood (thereby indicating to the other that he or she can once again expect him to be his old, more reserved self).

It immediately becomes apparent that if someone wishes, for any of a number of narcissistic reasons, to arbitrarily change the temperature of the relationship without bothering to let the other know why--the working on and sharing of meaningful, dynamic relational fluctuations being, of course, a hallmark of intimacy--it is quite easy to do so. One has merely to follow the path of least resistance, accept the inevitable drop in the mood of the relationship without endeavoring to correct it, as is usually the case, and thereby will be able to secretly savor the predictable jolt that such provocatively mysterious cooling off is bound to deliver to the other's peace of mind.

Another method, besides following the path of least resistance, is to actively lower the temperature of the relationship (typically occurring after someone has suffered an unacceptable, real or imagined narcissistic injury). A popular way to do this is to start subtracting what Eric Berne once ingeniously called strokes (the classic stroke being the all-American "Hi", accompanied with a smile). First, it is determined how many strokes one has been customarily dispensing, and how many are expected; then--depending on the magnitude of the offense and the need for distance--the subtraction follows accordingly.

It is worth noting that Berne's strokes were meant to describe the attempt to maintain a kind of social homeostasis and were primarily used after an absence of contact as a means of displaying the appropriate enthusiasm upon reestablishing contact with someone whose presence was supposedly missed. By contrast, what we are talking about here refers to what might be termed the basic level of interpersonal intimacy that has been attained. From that perspective, the subtraction of mandatory strokes of social deference is only one way of dampening the relational intensity and complexity of the interaction (the unconscious aim in this case being to disengage or divorce the self and not just to sabotage the continuity of convenient social rapport).

For all of these reasons, to secretly cool off one's investment in the other is an especially potent and easily accessible power operation--in light of the fact that at almost every interpersonal moment an unconscious decision may be made by either or both parties as to whether the relational set point needs priming, and if so, whether or not it is worth the effort.

THE CONTROLLING PERSONALITY

One of the leitmotifs of therapy is the patient's fear that he or she will forever be unable to escape the clutches of an especially controlling parent, spouse, lover, friend or boss. Compounding the issue is that often the person--through the mechanism of identification with the aggressor--will have unconsciously internalized selective attributes of the dominating other. I am reminded of a patient, a very sensitive, insecure, aspiring young actress who spent hour after hour in therapy lashing out at a mother who she believed would thwart her at every turn: who did not seem to hide the fact that she preferred her older sister whom she unabashedly praised in her presence; who hardly listened when they spoke on the telephone and almost never made mention of any of her accomplishments; who grew impatient if her daughter would bring up a problem that could not be resolved with a minute's worth of conventional advice and who became enraged--instantly slamming the phone down on the receiver--at the slightest hint that there was something less than perfect about the quality of her mother's love.

Like many other young artists, this woman supported herself by working part-time as a telemarketer, a job that was supposed to provide the free time she would need to go on auditions. What my patient had not counted on was just how demanding her job would prove to be. As a telemarketer, which is a euphemism for a high pressure sales person, she was expected to call up people out of the blue, who did not want to be called, and by rigidly adhering to a prepared script, to rapidly sell them any of an arbitrary number of household products. She was to remain on the phone, going from customer to customer, for most of the sixty minutes of each hour of the five hour shift she happened to be working on, taking only minimal breaks in order to go to the bathroom or refresh herself with a drink of water.

To insure that the necessary self-control was being exercised, monitors would regularly patrol the telemarketers' glass-partitioned booths and check on the quantity of calls that had been made and, especially, the number of sales recorded. And on special occasions the owner herself, a proud, independent woman reputed to be a self-made millionaire, would personally make the rounds: carefully examining the productivity sheet of every telemarketer, watching the room like a hawk for infractions of company protocol, while periodically stopping to engage in self-conscious, contrived pleasantries calculated to lessen the palpable tension engendered by her visits.

When I asked my patient how she felt about these heavy-handed surveillance tactics--fully expecting she would be at least inwardly chafing at such corporate one-upmanship and hardly prepared for her instantaneous, heartfelt and somewhat awestruck retort, "She takes control right away"--I immediately realized that unconsciously she had internalized salient traits of her supposedly noxious take-charge mother. (It is perhaps one ironic measure of the power of the controlling personality that it can foster its incorporations in the other.)

What follows, in order to make this clearer, is a common profile, drawn from a number of patients I have worked with, of what is often taken to be a controlling personality:

Typically, the person seems intensely focused on what she wants and everything, including the needs of the other, are regarded as either means to an end or an obstacle to be overcome. Such tunnel-visioned singlemindedness can easily seem ruthless and inhuman in its disregard for everything outside of its ken, which in itself can be frightening and over time disempowering. The fact that the person is in headlong pursuit of the fulfillment of her aims cannot help but put the other on the defensive (the intuitive understanding that nothing you could want which is independent of the person's needs could possibly interest her, inhibits any budding desire to initiate contact). In its stead is a realization that there is no interpersonal space in which to pursue any personal satisfaction; the only thing left being to defend one's territory, try not to get pushed around and not lose anything one already has. The experience is akin to attempting to interrupt someone--who is plainly busy and working intently to finish something that is obviously important--in order to ask them something that has nothing to do with them.

The controlling personality, therefore, characteristically seems more clear-headed, goal-oriented and no-nonsense than most people, as though they have a head start on you; as though all issues of ambivalence, uncertainty, self-doubt, and identity confusion have been at least temporarily surmounted or suspended. Since the majority of us rarely feel this way and less so in the company of another--where, although we may know what we want, we can never be sure of the other's intention--this can be daunting. We are intimidated by someone who takes it for granted they are more serious than we are and appears to be challenging us to say quickly whatever is on our minds.

It immediately becomes apparent that abruptness is a salient characteristic of the controlling personality. The message being unconsciously sent is that--in an analogous psychic sense--they are hurrying to catch a train and you are in their way.

If this is so, the question becomes--what is the effect on the other to be controlled in this fashion?

1.   Typically there is an almost instantaneous narcissistic injury accompanying the realization that someone would want to do this to you, would have so little appreciation of your attributes, that the very best use of you they can think of is to only and thoroughly exploit you.

2.   There is a simultaneous sense of being profoundly misunderstood. It is startling to perceive that someone could actually believe they could get away with such treatment, that you might possibly find it acceptable, or worse, that they were basically indifferent to your opinion of the matter. If that were the case, it could only be because they had no idea of who you were as a person.

3.   There is the creation of an immediately adversarial relationship. From that point on--even if the person superficially complies due to perception of the other's greater force of personality or power (e.g., being your boss)--the interaction will be characterized by attempts to control, followed by efforts to counter-control, which trigger renewed attempts to control, and so on. In such a transaction where each is struggling to win power over the other, it is instructive to note everything that is left out and that now seems to both parties to be utterly beside the point: empathy, the need to relate, be intimate, spontaneous, playful, expressive, to be understood. Every impulse to be decent goes out the window. It is as though

all possibilities or memories of the pleasure that one person can take in the company and presence of another have dried up or been forgotten.

It is obvious the creation of an adversarial relationship can have immediate consequences. If one can only expect a kind of psychic warfare vis-á-vis the other, it makes sense to raise one's guard, tune up one's defenses, trot out one's strategies and gamesmanship. This is a description, of course, of a competitive relationship, but a competition without the saving graces of mutual respect and appreciation of your opponent's prowess (as in professional sports at its best).

Inasmuch as the controlling personality usually vehemently denies that she or he is being controlling, the person cannot help but come across as profoundly dishonest in the way they are relating. Not only does the other, therefore, feel devalued by the manner in which she is being treated, but, as a violent counter-reaction, almost instantly loses respect for the controlling personality. It is a short step from this to feeling hated by the person--who is not only horribly mistreating you but is lying about it--to vigorously hating the person back, however secretly, and to thereby being subject to paranoid fears of being exposed for one's covert psychic malevolence.

For all of these reasons, someone who has characterologically learned to depend upon the secondary gains which derive from being a controlling personality will find reinforcements both in the other's compliance and in society's glorification of the successful uses of behavioral power--and will have scant motivation to give it up.

"YOU LOOK SCARY"

Andy is a tall, lanky, absent-minded graduate student who enjoys daydreaming while he rides the subway training, which may be the reason he is oblivious to the young man, dressed like a manual laborer, his arms wrapped around a large, upright board balanced against his knees, who is seated at right angles to him. It is only when the train rather abruptly lurches to a stop--causing the man and his board, reeling forward, to bang into Andy--that he is recalled from his reverie. Now he cannot help but notice the round youthful face, with the startled, contrite look about eight inches from his own and he certainly feels the board colliding with his right arm.

"I'm sorry," whispers the man, pulling the board to his chest and gently easing himself back into his seat. Whether emboldened by the crooning apologetic tone of voice, or simply irritated at being physically rousted from the privacy of his thoughts, Andy--glancing briefly but sharply at his intrusive neighbor--does not bother to hide his annoyance.

"You look scary."

Although apparently the same voice from the same young man of just a moment ago, the subtle change of intonation--now not even faintly solicitous--and

64

the change of expression--now devoid of emotion and utterly still--are enough to be menacing.

Unwilling to accept his feeling of vague but inexplicable threat, Andy, turning to his right, but making sure to be safely civil, decides to check on what he just heard, "Excuse me?"

And bending slightly forward, as though to make sure his words and message were accurately delivered the second time, the young man repeats, "You look scary." For a few seconds, Andy studies the expressionless face, searching for clues, and waiting, hoping, for an explanation that does not come. He feels his heart begin to beat more rapidly. Quickly he averts his eyes from the young man seated to his right and tries to act as though whatever did happen is over with. But clearly something is wrong. Although he does not dare to look, he can sense that he is being stonily stared at.

For the next ten minutes, as they ride together-- mute, motionless and in tandem--on the subway train, Andy agonizes over the meaning of those three little words. Could they have been intended literally? Could the man--perhaps overreacting to his initial flash of annoyance--have been trying to convey that he had been really somewhat intimidated? If so, then why grimly repeat himself, why stonily stare, why sit motionlessly in a kind of statuesque rage? No, reasoned Andy unhappily, those were fighting words, taunting words. What had begun in an effort to conciliate ("I'm sorry") had ended in sadism: "You look scary" plainly being meant as the mocking threat, "I am supposed to be afraid of you?"

In the session that followed the incident Andy spoke about the seemingly bottomless depths of his subsequent humiliation. He had been bumped fairly hard by a board while innocently minding his own business. He had not protested the jarring impact and slight injury except perhaps for a tiny display of understandable irritation. He had been forthwith challenged to a physical fight. He had been gracious enough to let this pass and allow the offender to regain his composure and act civilly. He had been once again challenged to fight. Now he had had no choice--short of engaging in mayhem in a public place--but to keep his head down, his face burning with shame, to swallow his pride and hope that no one else was witness to his degradation.

Although Andy's account of what happened had seemed quite plausible, as his therapist, I could not be sure of the underlying motives of the man who accosted him on the subway. In spite of that, it is fairly certain that probably millions of times daily in our country one person will intend not only to degrade another, but to rub his nose in it. This, of course, is simply an instance of what has been discussed as the desire to humiliate the other but so extreme that, in most cases, the perpetrator is both aware of and vindictively proud of his intention.

Typically, as it did with Andy, it will precipitate a full-blown crisis of self-esteem in the victim. On the one hand to not respond and meet the challenge head-on--instead taking flight into oneself and letting fear of the person's shocking aggression win the day--is to pave the way for unending self-recrimination and flagellations. On the other hand, to resist or refuse to be intimidated is to enter a dangerous no-man's land, to go one on one with someone who has willfully chosen to defy one of the strongest social taboos--never try to take away every vestige of the other's dignity. Only someone in an extraordinarily aggressive mood would dare to be that provocative. Since such aggression therefore seems almost unnatural, to realistically contest it would seemingly require a comparable amount of abnormally intense aggression.

But it is just this--because intentional humiliation is almost always experienced traumatically as a shock to the psyche, no matter how much it has occurred in the past or how anxiously anticipated--that the victim cannot do. Much more likely is that he will embrace an involuntary, although markedly defensive posture. Reinforcing his retreat will be the dread that--inasmuch as he cannot now imagine that he could have possibly provoked or deserved the inhuman abuse he is receiving-- should be change his mind and decide to go on the attack, the other may very well go berserk.

He is thus caught between a rock and a hard place: between the prospect of being annihilated and the prospect of everlasting shame. Although he does not use these words, the victim typically thinks that only someone possessed of psychotic hatred would want to thrust him in such an agonizing existential dilemma. While, by contrast, it seems clear the aggressor-- regardless of how pathologically sadistic he may be--could not live with his debasement of his victim unless on some level there were a projective identification of the other as one who is obviously and consummately despicable.

What makes this so painful for both parties is that two people who experience each other as almost alien beings--a transactional rupture of empathy so profound that it borders on a temporary psychosis--are nevertheless locked together in an intensely passionate, if adversarial interaction. (It is no small part of the seductive pull of the sadomasochistic contract--which itself can be looked upon as a defense against fears of engulfment and symbiosis--that it seems to offer a way to be fiercely bonded with another, while still being totally uncommitted.

Finally, adding to the pain of the one who has been humiliated, is what might be called the memorial power of shame: to be unable to defend oneself or at least try to against a brazen attempt to deliberately degrade one is to incur a sense of shame which few people are likely to forget. It is this ability to instill a psychic trauma with just a single act that lends it such a mesmerizing aura of power in the eyes of both the victim and sadist.

"AND IN THIS CORNER. . . ."

The antithesis, of course, to passively swallowing the other's sadism is to combat it. Invariably, this leads to a fight which--if the participants are sufficiently aggressive--can become physical. It is clarifying, however, to contrast this kind of an everyday, unstructured fight with a professionally regulated one, the clearest example of which is a prize fight where:

Two supposedly evenly matched opponents who are both well prepared choose to enter the ring. This in itself is frightening: that someone who has had a lot of time to think it over, who is not being provoked in any way by his opponent to fight, who can pursue other activities, nevertheless wants to go into the ring. It must mean he has an extraordinary capacity to cope with the anxiety associated with doing something that is truly dangerous. This is why, regardless of what one may think of the brutality and inhumanity of two men trying to literally knock one another unconscious, the physical courage required to enter and survive in the ring is widely admired.

Not surprisingly, in light of the great risk entailed in consenting to engage in a prolonged encounter with a presumably equally skilled, professionally trained prizefighter, numerous precautions--pre-fight physical, cut-men, ringside doctor and so on--are taken. Perhaps the greatest precaution, however, is that it is decreed that it is a contest that has to be fought according to rules, rules which will govern every aspect of the encounter: the size and construction of the gloves, weight of the fighters, length of the round, rest period, number of rounds, how they are to be scored, what type of blows are to be considered fair or foul, what parts of the opponent's body are to be considered legitimate targets for attack, what parts of one's own body can be used for striking the other (for example, the shoulders, forearm, elbows, knees, feet, the back of the hand, the head and the teeth are all disallowed).

How important these regulations are can be seen by how even seemingly the most savagely aggressive fighter will welcome the bell signalling the end of a given round and beginning of a mandatory rest period--at which point they will often touch gloves--and, especially, the bell signalling the end of the fight where it is customary, even after the most brutal of ring wars, for the warriors to embrace one another, openly proclaiming admiration and affection for the prowess and courage of their opponent, regardless of the outcome.

If one now compares this to a fight with a stranger in the street, it immediately becomes apparent there are no rules governing the fray--as rules in order to exist and be adhered to need to be recognized and agreed upon in advance. Although two strangers who get into a fight in the street will, of course, each have a particular style of fighting reflecting the level of aggression with which they are comfortable, what matters is that that style will not be known to their opponent. One of the things, therefore, that makes a street fight so very dangerous is that, other than an intuitive first impression of the kind of adversary their antagonist is likely to be, a person really has no reliable idea of what they are getting into. Is one merely standing up to someone who is only upset, but has no honest intention of seriously hurting the other? Or is the person an experienced, expert and (unfortunately) vicious street fighter, someone who looks forward to and savors beating an opponent to a pulp? An altercation with a stranger is dangerous, therefore, because it transcends the known rules of civilized agreement and disagreement where--although allowance is made for numerous unpleasantries to occur--there is an implicit guarantee that, assuming the person plays by the rules, not only will he get through trying situations, but that he will emerge in good shape.

By contrast, in a street fight, rules as such--which do not exist beforehand--will have to be improvised on the spot. The difficulty in doing this will depend in no small part on the difficulty in determining who is to be the aggressor and who is to be the defender. (From this standpoint, a sadist can be defined as someone who has mastered a certain technique for managing the potential trauma of a power struggle over who is to be humiliated, and a victim as someone who has not. In such a contest, the humiliator truly will typically have considerable experience upon which to fall back, while the designated victim, more likely than not, will have only fantasy--such as one's picture of what it might be like to be arrested for the first time. This may be why the sadomasochistic contract in order to sufficiently manage the potential for traumatic humiliation so as to enjoy the sexual arousal that is at least one aim--relies on ritualization (e.g., see Khan's, 1979, technique of perversions). Another way to say this is that, although there may be unwritten rules which govern the encounter, the victim is much less likely to know them than the sadist.)

It is instructive to compare fighting between human beings with that of other animals. As Konrad Lorenz (1966) has noted, when an animal, such as a wolf or lion, is heavily armed so that it is easily capable of killing a vanquished rival, natural selection provides an instinctive inhibition against so doing. Thus, the killing bite of the lion is almost never released while fighting with another lion and the wolf that is being thoroughly beaten by another has only to bare the most vulnerable part of its throat to insure--no matter how enraged its opponent may be--that it will not be killed. In that case, the message seems to be: "See how helpless I am, how easily you could kill me. You have nothing to fear, there is no danger coming from me." By contrast, with animals such as human beings who are not biologically armed (e.g., no fangs, or weapons to be selected against) there has been no evolutionary need, again according to Lorenz, to provide an innate inhibition when it comes to killing conspecifics. What this means is that there is no comparable instinctual check against killing one another in human beings as there is in lions and wolves.

One other difference concerns time. Fights among animals tend to be concrete, non-psychological and biologically driven. Everything else being equal, the stronger party usually wins and when they are over they tend to be over. By contrast, in humans--since you cannot control the psyche as easily as you can the body-- fights tend to last longer, or rather their aftermath is longer.

In spite of this, power operations characteristically are transacted quickly and are as opportunistically abrupt as possible. There is therefore a sense, in which no one fights fair: i.e., each party, even if contending within the parameters of the rules, is unconsciously looking for a power advantage. It follows, in the case of altercations that are markedly anti-social, such as a street fight, they will be manifestly unfair and this will apply to even the most decent person who, entirely against his will, has been forced into a position of justifiable self-defense. Fairness goes out the window as soon as a power struggle beings to escalate in the direction of a frank physical confrontation. By being unfair, I am not referring to someone who resorts to so-called dirty or foul tactics; I am using the term fair not as it is customarily employed in professional sports--where the concepts of fair and foul play exist as a primitive polarity primarily defined by arbitrary but enforceable rules which, in practice, means one does everything one can to manipulate and bend the rules so long as one does not get caught (e.g., if you're not caught, you're not cheating)--but in the therapeutic sense of displaying a decent regard and empathic consideration for the rights, feelings and needs of another person with whom one happens to be in genuine conflict.

In light of what has already been said about how parents' modus operandi is often to bully and practice tough love with their children upon the first whiff of discord, it is unrealistic to expect the abstract concept of fairness to counterbalance the dynamics of actual power operations other than to provide a reassuring sense that agreed-upon boundary points exist beyond which unrestrained bullying by someone who holds the upper hand cannot proceed without incurring definite peer pressure and social censure. Another way to say this is that there is no viable role model at present to be culled from our familial upbringing, general education or society at large vis-a-vis the concept of fairness when it comes to power operations.

If the concept of fairness is a social palliative, we may be more at the mercy of power operations then we would like to think. If so, it may be clarifying to look at--How Rules Regulate Behavior:

1.   Perhaps foremost is that they set limits. They do not directly affect the dynamics, quality or the flavor of the interaction. To return to our boxing analogy, they determine which actions are to be considered fair or foul.

2.   Rules are the antithesis of role models. They are indifferent to anything that happens short of the no trespass sign. Up until that point, you can do anything you like. In other words, rules are not interested in and do not relate to anything and everything that exists within the rules. It is only behavior that threatens to go beyond the borders of permissible actions that draws their attention. It follows rules have a negative, policing function and are therefore strictly about power--the maintenance and enforcement of power and the punishment of those who violate it.

This is particularly evident in the realm of professional sports in which contact is allowed. The most brutal punishment can then be meted out by one contestant to another, so long as the game is being played by the rules and, ironically, when this is the case and there results the occasional tragic death in the ring or the spinal cord injury on the football field, the predictable public outcry is not for the game to be played less savagely but for the rules to be changed.

3.   A policeman is an excellent example of the principle of a rule made

incarnate. So long as a law has not been broken or is not about to be broken, he does not care how or even whether people live or die. It is as though his interest in a given interpersonal field can only become animated around the pre-determined boundaries of a regulation, the taboo place where there is perhaps the greatest opportunity and temptation to violate a law. The flip side of this, of course, and an important unconscious secondary gain, is that rules also exist in order to show where lawlessness--the freedom to be as wanton, unrestrained, narcissistically empowered, greedily ambitious and controlling as one dares and, on the positive side, to be as expressive of the true self as one wants--can be practiced with impunity.

4.   In spite of which, it is obvious that, typically, rules, in their near-total self-absorption, function narcissistically, but it is a particularly potent form of narcissism because it is backed by real power.

Now to return to how fairness is used in a power struggle. Not, as mentioned, in the sense of an empathic and decent regard for the rights and needs of the other with whom one is locked in conflict but in the form of rules as used in sports. A fair fight, then, would be one in which both parties showed a healthy knowledge of and obedience to mutually agreed-upon rules designed to guarantee a level playing field. Again, as stated, one of the greatest dangers presented by the prospect of a street fight breaking out is the impossibility of trusting with any reasonable degree of confidence that the rules for fighting fairly between strangers are going to meaningfully coincide.

It becomes immediately apparent that a primary reason rules exist is to indicate the kinds of behavior that--because they too are deemed too dangerous to the self or harmful and vicious to others--are to be prohibited. Rules are therefore reassuring in that they tell you what cannot happen. They also tell you what will happen in terms of the things you must do in order to comply with them (thereby helping to structure your life). By telling you what cannot happen and what must happen rules imply that the persons or authorities that instituted them have the power to enforce them. However, in order for this to be in fact true, the force authorizing the rule must prove greater than the force resisting it.

In Bion's terms (1970) it could be said that part of the seductive appeal of rules is that they promise a container that will not crack under pressure. Much as one may loathe being restrained when one does not want it, there is comfort, especially during times of emotional turbulence, to know that limits exist (giving hope that turbulence will come to an end). In the unconscious may be this equation: rules = limits = termination = discharge/closure/resting.

Finally, for all of these reasons, the fear of getting into a fight which one would much rather avoid, or of losing a fight, can be traumatizing. It follows the power one has is most effective when it is feared. This is the secret the bully knows well--and from that perspective, it could be said that the power that is not feared is not power. Which is why it is such an efficient regulator of the other's behavior. Once feared, it does not have to be used, thereby saving enormous energy: e.g., the average policeman who almost never uses his gun, because he doesn't have to. The consolidation of power, therefore, will characteristically be the product of only a few traumatic encounters in which the superiority of one's forces was indelibly impressed upon one's adversary. This may be why childhood memories of one's worst bullies typically tend to be quite meager, in spite of the fact that the narcissistic injuries incurred can be quite persuasive.

It is yet another reason why power struggles, especially intense ones, almost invariably aim for the knockout blow. The message being clear: if you choose to challenge me, you will not only lose, but lose traumatically.

BLUFFING

The analogue in humans for the variety of physiological mechanisms and adaptations--the lion's mane, markings around the eyes, baring of fangs--which exist in the animal kingdom for the express purpose of tricking their enemies or rivals into thinking they are bigger or fiercer than they really are, is the interpersonal strategy of bluffing: the art of making the other believe, in short, that one has more power than one does.

Dynamics Of Bluffing

1.   Perhaps the key underlying assumption is that one cannot trust that one has sufficient resources to realistically confront a perceived threat. By simple projection there is the fear that the would-be opponent can not only see this, but be emboldened by it, thereby becoming even more of a threat. The most logical alternative then is to engage in what Erving Goffman (1959) has called impression management--trying to disguise and compensate for inner defects by the presentation of an attractively cohesive, imposing and, if necessary, threatening front.

2.   Bluffing implies there is no honest backup, no intention to stand behind what one appears to be saying and doing. It follows bluffing not only compensates for its hidden defects but also for its undeniable lack of sincerity and commitment. Since the bluff by definition is in what Sartre has called bad faith, it runs the risk of being exposed at any moment (by being called) and it therefore unconsciously strives to achieve its counterfeit aim as quickly as it can. Another way to say this is that the bluffer is typically in a hurry to win his bluff because he generally feels time is not his ally. The bluff, therefore, tends to be larger than life-- not in the physical sense of the lion's mane--but rather in the gestural sense of being (what they call in acting) too big a gesture. Because of this, the bluff is not just an exaggeration, enhancement and advertisement of one's strength. It is also, to the extent that it impersonates another presumably more powerful persona, an abandonment of the true self. The result is something even less authentic than a false self: an impersonation.

3.   When successful, bluffs, like instilling the fear of power, are psychic energy savers. They can influence the behavior of the other without having to invest much of themselves. It is obvious, however, for someone to have a successful career as a bluffer it is important to be able to back up the bluff when it is called. Bluffs, in other words, work best when they are not perceived as bluffs. Which is why bullies, when challenged, if they can, like to administer a serious beating to their critics: the message being--"Don't every make the mistake of thinking that I am bluffing."

There is a myth that bullies are often bluffing, that they are afraid to pick on someone of equal strength and cannot stand the pressure of a fair contest. The kernel of truth in this perception is not that bullies are afraid of a good fight--real bullies love to fight-- but that they find losing unbearable (because of a defect in their self, which they are anxiously trying to compensate for by an orchestrated show of strength in something at which they are quite good). And since bullies unconsciously know they cannot tolerate a loss, they look for an edge, such as a weaker opponent or someone who appears to be afraid of them. The fact they sometimes collapse spectacularly upon losing is a reflection of their fear of the humiliation of losing and not their fear of the pain of combat.

I think this is amply borne out, for anyone who follows violent contact sports such as boxing and football, by the biographies of contemporary star players: wherein some of the most physically fearless and brutally tough athletes in the history of the game will often confess how, as youngsters--driven by broken, abusive homes or feelings of deprivation and inferiority, yet also sensing an awesome physical power--they would take it out on other youngsters, perceived as more socially advantaged, by savagely bullying them. From this perspective, it could be said that one possibly socially redeeming value of dangerous professional contact sports is that they channel the destructive energies of incorrigible bullies into safe conduits, providing undreamed-of substitutive rewards and recognitions, and thereby displacing the need to discharge their hostility directly upon innocent people. In other words, a secondary gain of violent contact sports--from the standpoint of society--is that it stops some of its more efficient and talented physical predators from running loose in the streets. Although one could not prove it, it is hard to imagine--if one looks at the incredible aggression that is released and more or less dissipated in the arena of big-time professional contact sports--how such animalistic emotions could be similarly curbed in the everyday world without comparable, socially sanctioned rechannelling, accompanied by unprecedented rewards. (As a simple thought experiment, think of the most mythically tough, fiercely combative sports icon you admire and then picture the probable course of their life if they had failed to be drafted into professional sports.)

4.   Depending on the underlying motivation, there are two kinds of bluffs: (1) the one born of panic, when the person is usually on the brink of being exposed, humiliated or harmed and (2) the one born of manic confidence--the bluff,

that is, of the seasoned poker player, corporate or street bully who knows how to and enjoys instilling feelings of inferiority and insecurity in the other.

Interpersonal Examples of Everyday Bluffing:

1.   Q. (from a policemen) "What are you doing?"

A. (from a startled pedestrian) "Is there a problem officer?" The person pretends to be someone who is utterly unperturbed, with nothing to fear, and not someone who, regardless of his innocence, is typically terrified of the policeman's power.

2.   Q. (from an insecure, suspicious wife) "Do you ever think of having an affair?"

A. (from a guilty husband) "Of course not." Here, a married man who--while perhaps not seriously entertaining the idea, but who has fantasized countless times about what it would be like to once again share in the swinging, hedonistic pleasures of his bachelor friends--is caught off guard. Feeling unable to or uneasy about responding truthfully (which may or may not upset or threaten his wife) he concocts an answer and a persona which he wants to believe cannot fail to impress and satisfy her.

It follows at the unconscious moment of the decision to pretend, the anticipated compromise of his authentic self will tend to seem acceptably expedient. When the discrepancy, therefore, between the power the person thinks he has and the power he imagines is necessary to handle the other is substantial enough, a bluffing transaction will occur. Put another way, a bluffing transaction is one in which the person makes no attempt whatever to express, in even an attenuated way, his true self but, instead, forsaking it, opts to present a makeshift persona that is designed strictly according to perceived power needs.

This is especially confusing in everyday life where one is not ordinarily subject to role-regulations and where therefore it is usually unclear as to how much expression of the self, opposed to a show of power, is expected or required. The person can then be susceptible to guilt that he may be shortchanging himself by investing too much in conveying a favorable impression. By contrast, there is considerably less existential guilt over this issue when the person is enacting a role that is transparently based on power: i.e., being a boss, policeman or soldier. When that is the case, the bluff as such is incorporated into the structure of the role once typically manifested in the uniform where the intent is plainly to enhance the natural image. In itself this can be intimidating--delivering the message that "most of my resources are going into the maximization of my power which, if necessary, can be focused on constraining you". Although conflicts over the usage of power which come up in the enactment of a rule--because they have been well defined and sanctioned beforehand--tend to be expedited rather quickly, tensions concerning the thwarted needs of the self are more likely to be denied, suppressed or ignored.

Perhaps the most common bluff in today's power-oriented society is to deny being either emotionally or intellectually vulnerable:

Thus (to someone visibly upset):

Q.   "Were you frightened?" or "Were your feelings hurt?"

A.   "Not at all."

And (to someone plainly confused):

Q.   "Do you understand?"

A.   "Yes."

In our information-infatuated age people almost universally feel overwhelming pressure--in order to be accepted and respected--to pretend to have access to far more data than they in fact have or is really possible for any one person to have. In turn this gives rise to some of the dynamics of interpersonal bluffing: where (as noted by Goffman) unconsciously people understand that one of the primary collusive aims of social interaction is to allow all participants in good standing to bathe themselves in a better light than they deserve providing, of course, they do not abuse it by asking for too much or by really expecting the other to literally take them at their word and treat them accordingly. Goffman (1957) gives the example of the host who customarily acts as though she is willing to extend every conceivable hospitality to her guest on the condition, of course, that she is not taken up on it and asked to do more than the required minimum. Another way to put this is that a large part of being social entails politely looking the other way whenever one realizes the other is bluffing vis-à-vis his or her self image (providing one's own self-interests are not thereby adversely affected). This may be due to the almost universal social habit of endeavoring to wear an appropriate mask whenever we are interpersonally perceived. And from the standpoint of our theme we can add that when it is issues of the self and not of the social persona, it is nearly inevitable, and second nature, to try to assume a mask of power whenever we feel misunderstood, mistreated or in any way threatened.

Finally, there is the sense in which all defense mechanisms--intrapsychic and interpersonal--can be thought of as bluffs, not only to the other, but to the self as well. Defenses, after all, characteristically operate as though they are working in concert without a hitch and are up to handling any contingency. Ironically defenses--which by definition are the result of defensiveness--tend to deny that they themselves may be the product of or affected by the very same conflict that they have been constructed to attenuate or resolve. From an object relational point of view, it could be said that defenses are born of mistrust: sought out when there is little hope of the self being satisfied or nurtured by relating to the other. Defense means defense against real or imagined threat and attack. They can be thought of as psychic armor. To arm oneself means to mobilize one's resources of power, such as a facility for instilling fear in the other through the art of bluffing.

It is therefore part of the definition of power operations that it will try to appear more powerful than it really is. Accordingly, power has no use for the true self, much preferring to believe in the efficacy of facade and impression, specifically as it impacts on the other. Which is why someone who is being non-intimate--

except perhaps when making a point of being aggressively hostile--will typically try to bluff the other into thinking he feels more intimate than he does, if only because it is so painful for both parties to admit otherwise.

> "Cowards die many times before their deaths;
> The valiant never taste of death but once."

As a young psychotherapist I was sufficiently taken with Alfred Adler's powerful observation that it required courage to overcome the crippling effects of neurosis (1956) that I attempted to incorporate it into my so-called nascent technique. Whenever a patient, therefore, would show uncommon fortitude in facing up to an objectively harrowing emotional ordeal--especially someone who had a history of backing down and giving up in the face of psychic adversity--I would say, "That took courage." To my surprise, it proved a simple but surprisingly effective intervention. With few exceptions the patient was genuinely heartened, sometimes telling me afterwards they had never before been validated in that fashion in their lives. As a therapist I could not help but be impressed by the meaning that the attribution of courage held for my patients and from that point on began to study it in its own right.

Being courageous, I realized, implies that there is a part of oneself that one trusts will speak up for and, if necessary, fight to preserve certain elements of the self. This in turn implies that these elements are considered worthy enough to do battle over. Someone in touch, therefore, with their courageous self is likely to feel that excitement and the burst of energy that comes from the exercise of their healthy narcissism. There may be no more convincing sign of self-valuation than a display of bona fide courage on behalf of the true self. (As Christopher Bollas has noted, 1987, each of us has internalized a particular style of parental care which we then transfer onto the way we handle our own self as an object.)

One of the fondest memories of childhood and one of the safest times perhaps is when our parents were fighting, in a healthy sense, to protect us. It may, therefore, be that being courageous is, in some measure, a defense and denial that one is unloved, uncared for and not respected. This may partly explain why character disorders, sociopaths and borderline types--those who seem especially isolated, abandoned and impoverished in their object relations--so often prove to be fierce fighters on their own behalf, as though they would rather die (and they sometimes do) than let the shadow of dishonor fall on the self. In other words, by fighting so ferociously to protect their public reputation, they may be unconsciously striving to enact a primitive family romance of what it would be like to be jealously and parentally safeguarded; i.e., only a bloody, life-threatening struggle in which they are battling someone who is intent on seriously harming them, can convince them that at least someone would be deeply upset if they perished. In this way one can come to look upon one's courage, especially if it has been publicly demonstrated, as one's psychic bodyguard.

By contrast, if one has never really shown unquestionable courage, ambivalence concerning one's self-worth can only be reinforced. One may then wait for a test in which one can at last prove one's fortitude, as a necessary definition and validation of one's identity. One may feel that only certain courageous acts can lend a stamp of authenticity to other cherished values and attributes of the self. After all, it is almost universally believed a parent will risk himself for the child he loves. Contrarily, a lover who will take no chances to protect his or her love object from clear danger will not be considered much of a lover; while a solider who professes to love his country but who goes AWOL upon being called to battle, will not be considered much of a patriot. (Adam Phillips, 1996, has noted that one of the reasons mourning is so important is because it seems to prove to us that we really do need objects, and Wittgenstein, 1969, has remarked that no one seems to doubt the authenticity of someone who screams in pain). Analogously, showing courage may be significant in that it proves to us, by the risks we are willing to take, that certain values are indispensable.

Although we may sometimes call upon it, courage does not seem to be something under the auspices of the ego or will, a skill that one develops. Rather it is something that reveals itself, that one discovers or fails to discover--an unconscious reservoir of untapped resolve that rarely gets summoned into play except at moments of crisis. One waits for one's courage as one waits for another. (Of course, in contrast to the ordinary person there is the Man of Courage--for example, a professional daredevil--whose life is based on and fuelled by the dangers and risks to which his seemingly insatiable fund of courage expose him.)

Shakespeare's famous boastful hero, Julius Caesar, because he is imbued with courage, cannot be killed psychically by adversity. That is, if the hero, no matter how beleaguered and seemingly doomed, can always manage to find sanctuary in his courage--his seemingly endless resolve to fight on no matter what the odds against him--then literally he cannot be killed in spirit, but only in body. Instead, he dies only once--biologically. By contrast, the coward dies every time his courage fails him.

In this sense courage is a shield, a manic shield, against the fears of our own mortality. Paradoxically, if we have this fierce, self-protective love called courage, it can seem we can not die which, unconsciously, is what the excessively courageous person believes. On the other hand, if there is a manic element informing acts of courage, eventually there should be some kind of crashing and deflation. And this is what we see: even the bravest, seemingly invincible prizefighter, once beaten, can appear to be a different man. You might say, therefore, that the courageous individual can tolerate any adversity so long as he or she remains courageous: that is to say, does not feel fear, especially what is perceived as cowardly fear. Perhaps courage, because it is an expression of an extreme emotional state, has to psyche itself up and polarize itself--no half-way measures will do.

The Dynamics Of Being Courageous

Patients naturally report a variety of experiences associated with acts of courage. Here, however, are some common denominators that come into play when a person is acting and feeling courageous.

1.   Typically, the ordinary, non-heroic person tends to take a deep breath before undertaking something that is viewed as patently dangerous. Being courageous, then, can feel like letting go of a customary lifeline, and instead embarking on a kind of radical jumping off--psychically analogous to leaping off a diving board higher than one has ever encountered--into an uncharted territory of great risk. It can feel like a quantum leap from a familiar place equipped with a normal support system and a basic safety net to an area that has no safety net. The fact that the passage from being ordinary to courageous is so often discontinuous, with no transition whatsoever, can make it seem heady and exciting and, although it may appear obvious, it is worth noting that one important reason for being courageous is because one is intolerably bored or feeling deadened.

2.   To be courageous is also to have one's thoughts and emotions organized into a goal--as though one is fighting a common enemy of the different parts of the self. So long as one is engaged in courageous deeds, therefore, one does not need to struggle with an identity crisis. It feels good to be courageous because all of one's defenses will then be in play, due to the state of high arousal caused by the perceived danger, with the result one feels well defended, and therefore, paradoxically, very safe while, or course, simultaneously being uncommonly threatened. Such dynamic tension and dialectic--"Am I secure, powerful and about to be triumphant?" or "Am I recklessly imperiling myself and on the brink of being serious hurt?"--lend it its experiential soap operaish quality. There is probably no other time in our life when we feel we are living out a real life soap opera than when we act daringly.

3.   A person then feels uniquely honest, authentic (you are putting your money where your mouth is), self-revelatory, open and expressive. By showing what you most care about, put most stake in, need most to preserve and protect, you are showing a core part of one's true self values. There is therefore a sense of making contact, genuinely communicating and, in spite of the fact the other is often viewed as an opponent, to being somehow intimate.

4.   There is a feeling of rushing to a closure of some kind. Unless one is merely being stoical, such as bearing up to continuous deprivations (e.g., at a job one hates or in prison), an act of courage typically conveys a sense of imminence. And the end which is in sight, being primordial--will one survive, conquer, or go down and be humiliated?--more often than not comes quickly (at the conclusion of the combat or tribulation). It follows that characteristically there is the belief that something of immense importance to the individual is about to be determined.

For all of these reasons, being courageous can feel as though one is being idealistic. By risking a good part of what it has taken a lifetime to consolidate--a person's basic sense of security in the world--one shows dramatically that one is living by a code of conduct, an ethical sense of the terms on which life should be lived, that transcends the law of self-preservation. Herein lies the dignity of being courageous.

On another level, of course, being courageous, to the degree that it is a response to an extreme situation, can defer ongoing intimacy issues of the true self with the rationalization that one is dealing with a self-evidently meaningful situation (which renders everything else irrelevant). And, finally, being courageous, involving as it does great risk, involves great choice. If ever one doubted it, one is at last a true existentialist partaking in the Sartrian great NO. For doesn't one say NO to everything in oneself, to the other or the world which tries to persuade the person that it is wiser not to risk so much and to be far less courageous?

Relationship To Power

By definition, courage is the capacity not to lose heart in the face of being an underdog, being overmatched or unequipped to deal with a formidable opponent or obstacle. Put another way, it is the essence of courage that it strives not to submit to a transaction based on power, regardless of how superior that power may be. From the standpoint of the one in power, therefore, the courage of the other is a rebel or dissident that needs to be nipped in the bud. Thus it is that the bully, as mentioned, looks to punish as severely as possible any incipient show of bravado from a disgruntled victim, while the corporate higher-up will do everything to define it as an irrelevant, although disruptive personalization of a situation characterized by an admittedly inequitable distribution of power, but, nevertheless, one presumably based on merit.

For someone, therefore, who is intent on gaining his or her ends essentially be means of power, the courageous protest of the other is viewed primarily negatively--as resistance. As such, it is a stumbling block, a thorn in one's side. The clearest example of this, perhaps, is the policeman's attitude--bolstered by the fact that the law provides stiff penalties for anyone resisting arrest--to a show of defiance by someone who is in the process of being interrogated. From such a perspective, oppositional courage is no more than resistance to be overcome. What makes suicidal, kamikaze courage--the courage of a terrorist, hijacker or mad bomber who is willing to die--so terrifying is its ability to temporarily turn the tables and thwart overwhelming superior forces. (Which it does by revealing the weakness of entrenched power--that it depends on the other's submission, due to fear, and is not prepared for complete refusal to rationally acknowledge the likelihood of defeat. Because of this, it doesn't know what to do and is not prepared to handle the solitary fanatic or lunatic who does not happen to have any sane respect for its evident superiority of power.)

On the other hand, there is a curious relationship between the one who has power and their own courage. As mentioned, the person who wants to show power tends to move slowly, calmly, at their own pace, as though certain of the outcome of their actions, with as much fearless confidence in the rightness of what they are doing as can be mustered, independently of the responses or especially the needs of the other. From that standpoint, an act of courage, inasmuch as it is typically a manifestation of a fierce oppositionalism to a real or imagined adversary and to that extent is basically reactive, is incongruous with the autocratic, isolationist stance of the power broker. Furthermore, since courage, by definition, is a passionate acknowledgement of and attempt to surmount a plainly disadvantaged if not weakened position, it is incompatible with the one-upmanship overview of the power player. This is borne out in the respective differences in their styles of fighting: unlike the man or woman of courage who valiantly strives to overcome a frightening adversary, the person of power endeavors to merely smother, immobilize, crush or teach his opponent a much-needed lesson.

THE POLITICS OF RELATING

It is a characteristic of a transaction based on power that it endeavors to take as much and give as little as possible, to appropriate and, when necessary, to demand tribute. One way to accomplish this is to use the power of the structure that is conferred by the role definition to impress upon the subordinate other that they are indeed getting something, being a beneficiary just by brushing up against the person in charge, and that it may not be necessary to give anything else. The classic example of this in our society, as already indicated, is the American boss: where there is often the implicit expectation that you are grateful for the nearness, the availability and the security attached to the presence of the one on top (an attitude ridiculed in the old joke, "I'm going to give you something greater than a raise--my handshake!").

It follows from this that the person who has authority will hold in his hands a disproportionate share of the primary resources for getting the job done, that decisive action will not be reciprocal, does not depend on feedback, but flows in one direction only, from him at the hub outward to a field of group tension or concern. This carries with it a corollary assumption--that the subordinate other's contribution is secondary if not often useless. Which sets up a third assumption, that for the boss merely to interact with, include in any way in his actions, or take time out to answer a question of one of his underlings, is to give something of genuine value.

From the standpoint of giving and true nurturance, therefore, the transaction based on power, even when seriously pretending to be serving the other's needs, acting functionally or cooperatively, really believes it has only to be itself, to discharge and exercise its own power, in order to convince most outsiders that it is relating in an acceptable fashion (explaining why there is almost a universal, maddening sense of frustration by the recipients that their needs count hardly at all when in contact, especially, with officially entrenched, hierarchical power structures).

It is worth noting that when giving is from the hands of power it is almost always top-down, hierarchical, presumably originating from the highest point of either a psychical, familial, societal, business or social structure and then trickling down to a designated subordinate person, interaction or situation, less developed or advantaged, that is meant to be the beneficiary of its largesse. Thus, nurturance delivered from a position of authority is also essentially non-reciprocal, an aftermath which follows so seamlessly and insidiously from the fact that power operations are typically unilateral, that it is overlooked.

If this is so, what, then, is <u>hierarchical nurturance</u>? It means, among other things, that the giver gives not because he wants to or happens to be nurturing but because he is empowered with and under an obligation to distribute a substantial supply of services and goods. Whenever a seeming intent to nurture, therefore, travels along traditional hierarchical lines of power--a boss, for example, offering a generous group health insurance plan or a liberal allotment of paid vacation days to employees--it is usually almost impossible to disentangle and properly evaluate the two motives: the wish to show off and exercise power from the wish to authentically nurture the needs of the other.

The paradigm, of course, for confusion generated by hierarchical, non-reciprocal nurturance goes back to the family of origin. For how does the infant/child determine and sort out whether the parents who protect and provide do so basically because they are powerful or because they truly love him or her? The same basic ambiguity applies in even greater measure the further up one moves in one's development on the ladder of social services and support systems: can one ever tell if the educator, the physician, priest or policemen educates, treats, sermonizes or safeguards because they want to or have to? Parents, of course, like most people who are empowered, are not as perplexed on this issue as their children: the clear prestige and social sanction accorded to traditional enactments of hierarchical nurturance make it unnecessary to doubt the authenticity of the giving.

As opposed to this, as I am sure the reader is by now aware, I believe that true intimacy and nurturance, at least among adults, is fundamentally a bottom-up affair. It is conceived in the singularity of the moment, a reciprocal interaction spontaneously arising between two subjectivities having little or no need to borrow from or depend on the secondary benefits of hierarchical power.

On the other hand, hierarchical nurturance is not to be confused with genuine non-reciprocal nurturance: e.g., the parent who is in tune with her child's true self needs, loves her child for himself, and gives for the sheer joy of nurturing a growing self, which, although and because it occurs so rarely, is what I consider the highest form of intimacy. By contrast, hierarchical nurturance is basically about power which it officially denies with occasional gestures of pro forma recompense.

It follows that one way to escape from the ongoing constraints and complexities of reciprocal intimacy is to shift the focus from nurturance, which can be a long-term affair, to power, which at least in principle can be short and sweet-- that is to say, by politicizing the relationship. What does it mean to politicize a relationship? It means to put the experiential enactment of the interaction in brackets and to step back and concentrate on the various inequities in power, privileges and civil rights presumed to exist as a result of familial, societal, cultural and sexist stereotyping. The implicit assumption being that it is far more important to right what is politically wrong than it is to actually continue engaging in the relationship in its present depriving and unegalitarian form.

Thus, the relationship is diagnosed as politically sick and is quarantined, so to speak, until it can be, if not cured, at least put on the road to convalescence. From the standpoint of our theme, what is important is the underlying assumption that by aggressively focusing on the politics of the relationship--the vicissitudes of the dynamics generated by the inequities of power between the players--somehow one is being more nurturing to the other (supposedly by working to facilitate at some distant point in the future a more politically correct climate for interrelating) than if one was being honestly, empathically and personally giving in the here and now. In short, to politicize a relationship is not to have and not to be in one, but to compensate for this lack with the narcissistic empowerment that comes from dabbling in the politics of the self.

To politicize a relationship, therefore, means to endeavor to raise to consciousness certain interpersonal inequities, assumed to be sexist in origin and the by-product of large and devious social forces that, dangerously, are being taken for granted. In this sense to politicize means to introduce issues for political consideration, and hopefully revision, that hitherto were not considered grist for the political mill. (I discussed this in detail in my book, The Singles Scene, Alper, 1994.)

On the other hand, it is obvious, if we are talking not about the consciousness-raising vis-á-vis sexism that still flourishes on the singles scene--but about the interpersonal dynamics deriving from enactments of firmly established roles, that it is typical of the politics of power to deny that politics is involved. (Even in a presidential election, where the politics of power is most nakedly in view, it is customary for the candidates to repeatedly and categorically deny that the acquisition of political power, for the sake of power, is a motive for their feverish pursuit of the highest office in the land). Put another way, a power operation is one that tends to assume that any issues of active politicking over alleged inequities and abuses of rights have long ago been resolved (justly) in favor of the status quo and all that remains is to properly function according to the modus operandi. It is obvious this is particularly easy to do when one is operating under the umbrella of an institutionalized, societal, professional or business role, and is considerably harder to do when the field of action is the interpersonal one in which democratic values supposedly prevail (to then subtly or overtly control, influence or coerce the behavior of the other in such a presumably egalitarian context will require enough psychic force to merit the appellation 'power').

For all of these reasons, hierarchical nurturance is a handy avoidance of the challenge and demand of real giving. Once again the analogy to parent-child non-reciprocal giving is useful. It is so difficult for ordinary parents to satisfactorily discharge their obligations to their children in conformity to basic social and legal standards, to clothe, feed, house, educate, send to school, while keeping them on the approved developmental track without having to resort to visible abuse, that, having done so, it is natural to believe that they have performed rather admirably. Parents whose children are perceived as normal by those who are supposed to be able to judge them, understandably tend to take pride in their accomplishment. It is worth noting that no one really asks them, or seems to care, whether they have functioned as good parents because they have wanted to or felt they had to. And it follows that most parents who have suffered the ordeal of raising and disciplining children, who more or less have suitably adapted to the complexities of modern life, will not question themselves too carefully on this crucial point either. That they have not buckled under the weight of the extraordinary parental demands placed upon them, is more than enough.

By contrast, as mentioned, children instinctively will have almost no empathy for the rigors of being a parent unless, of course, they are in the hands of dysfunctional, abusive parents (e.g., alcoholics) who insist that they do. They will, however, be exquisitely sensitive to all those occasions when there is a plain conflict of interests and an ensuing power struggle, those times when their parents will retreat behind bullying, self-serving tactics. And they will resentfully note, especially at those instances when disciplinary punishment is being administered, how little empathy is really manifested for the suffering they are undergoing, the pain they are experiencing, and the deprivation they are being forced to endure.

Now to analogize this unique non-reciprocal, parent-child relationship to the world of adult power operations. One immediate difference is that parents, in spite of or because of the non-reciprocity, are expected to be empathic, whereas consenting adults (unless in the so-called helping professions) who are engaged in inequitable power transactions are not realistically expected to be empathic. The availability and exercise of their power in a functional way--for example, dispensing necessary information or services in howsoever a lordly manner--is considered nurturance enough. Typically, analogous to the parents' overview of how much is required just to minimally discharge their responsibilities, the person who thinks he or she is in charge, in fact or fantasy, aware of what it takes to acquire, maintain and wield power, tends to be quite satisfied with doing that and only that. Hence, the flourishing of hierarchical nurturance. And finally, analogous to parent-child interaction, the person perceiving himself on the short end of the stick will be attuned, despite any and all secondary benefits accruing from the exercise of superior authority (it is, of course, the essence of intimacy that the nurturance is never derivative of power operations) that the transaction is profoundly self-serving.

PERFORMING FOR LOVE

In the ideal parent-child relationship, the child is valued for his or her self and does not have to pay back the parents for all their non-reciprocal sacrificing by performing. The child is not required to earn love, but receives it just by being.

But, even so, taking this ideal to the extreme, when is the point when a parent's non-reciprocal acceptance of a delinquent child's seemingly complete lack of interest in autonomously investing in the worth of the attachment by working to enhance it--not by performing for parental approval or to gratify narcissistic parental needs, but in a child's way (enriching the bond as he or she sees fit)--become instead outright abuse at the hands of their children? To put it another way, if it is to be a viable, non-destructive relationship the child needs to reciprocate, not equally, but in some phase-appropriate, meaningful fashion. It is probably true, therefore, that so-called unconditional love does not exist (at least not after the period of primary maternal identification and resulting infantile omnipotence as described by Winnicott, 1965).

When we come to consenting adults, however, where intimacy is supposed to be an achievement and project of two people, the same question becomes considerably more complicated, but no less pressing. At what point, when simply allowing the one who is loved to be--where such being manifestly does not seem to reflect in any way an awareness of the existence of the self of the other--does it become abusive indifference at the hands of the beloved? And at what point does our request, or demand in the face of narcissistic withdrawal that the loved one pay attention and relate to us begin to become--not an overture for closeness--but coercion? What is important here is not that there can be no clear answers to such questions, but the implicit understanding informing them that in mature love the ability to work on the inevitable conflict of interests and resulting interpersonal tensions is an indispensable indication of the underlying psychic investment. In other words, in the unconscious work can be a proof of love.

It is worth noting that working on behalf of the best interests of both partners in the service of mutuality is a far cry from performing in order to gain approval and affection as a reward for gratification of the other's narcissism. A healthy adult relationship, therefore, whether personal or professional, always involves some reciprocity. The average employee, for example, does not have a reciprocal say with his boss regarding what, when, and how he is to work. But this obvious inequity in autonomy is at least partially balanced by another inequity--the non-reciprocal economic arrangement in which the exchange of monies travels only one way, from the employer to the employee. Thus, the oft-noted non-reciprocal nature of the therapeutic situation is somewhat compensated for by the fact that the therapist works primarily in the service of facilitating the patient's difficulties in living, but makes no such request in return. Of course, two inequities do not make an equal, whole relationship. (In the next chapter, I discuss the consequences of the various inequities in the therapeutic situation.)

It is important that in a power transaction, by contrast the work that is done is not considered a sign of underlying intent to nurture and to relate, but a measure instead of the skill, resources and determination of the person. What counts is the end result, the bottom line, who gets to use what and whom. In a power transaction, the prestige one has, how one can influence or, if necessary, perform for the other become meaningful, superseding how one relates.

PSEUDO AUTONOMY

Today it is fashionable to talk about pseudo intimacy, as though we know what intimacy is. But what about pseudo autonomy, which we rarely hear about? This may be defined as a sense of independence that is based--not on the ability to express and actualize the deepest needs of the true self--but on the instrumentality, efficacy and capacity of the false self to impact on, manipulate and control the other.

Pseudo autonomy, therefore, is a feeling of power, bolstered by the illusion that psychic force is tantamount to freedom. This, of course, is not to deny that having power thereby grants one a certain freedom not to be intruded upon, easily discounted or restrained in the familiar way that others are and to be able to say, pretty much whenever one wants, with impunity, "Don't tell me what to do." It is a freedom to be able to gratify, rather than actualize or express oneself, to acquire and appropriate, rather than to relate.

So it is no accident that some of our most obnoxious and abrasive talk show hosts are also some of our noisiest libertarians. In other words, pseudo autonomy unconsciously goes hand in hand with political power, political autonomy, what might be called the civil rights and libertarianism of the self. At its root is the angry, obsessive and sometimes paranoid assertion that almost no one has the right to tell him what to do, in spite of the fact that he often blatantly lords it over everyone he considers less politically enlightened.

Pseudo autonomy, therefore, tends to be based on visible displays and outer versus inner power. It is more dependent on an other from whom it can pretend to act conspicuously independent. It gravitates towards the social. It obsessively seeks and needs validation of its identity from others, unlike genuine autonomy which works privately and unconsciously within the domain of the self. Not surprisingly pseudo autonomy is fond of recharging and reinventing itself with a kind of pop existentialism, the favorite motto of which is, "Life is about choices."

It is obvious there is something heady about feeling empowered, to believe that people cannot push you around because they fear you. The illusion is to believe that because they fear you, they respect you. What is then overlooked is that there

84

is a difference between political freedom and what Christopher Bollas (1995) has termed unconscious freedom: i.e., as history has repeatedly shown, someone can be desperately driven, and psychically constricted, yet have awesome political power. The difference coming down, perhaps, to that between action-mobility (Goffman, 1967) and psychic fluidity.

The flip side of pseudo autonomy is that it tends to be all or nothing and cannot admit, because it cannot integrate, its own dependence and vulnerability. IN therapy, the classic example is the patient who can only feel free if he leaves a relationship and is no longer in contact with his need for another. He or she must feel self-contained and self-sufficient in order to feel independent. To feel truly differentiated, he or she needs to be unrelated to the other.

Finally, pseudo autonomy is an excellent defense against the fragile, dependent psychic elements underlying the stance of power. From the standpoint of intimacy, if I had only one word to characterize an interpersonal transaction essentially based on power, it would be 'hollow'. At its core, it is constituted not so much by its anti-human or malignant intention but rather by its profound absence of any redeeming, vital humanism. It is as though the person who has really committed himself or herself to a power play, whether situationally or characterologically, has entered a kind of dead zone in which values of empathy, compassion, spontaneity, playfulness and intersubjectivity simply do not exist, having been displaced by the absorbing, animating and earnest pursuit of pseudo-autonomous self-aggrandizement.

By underscoring the hollowness when it comes to human relatedness, it is not meant to imply that such a person is anything less than formidable when locked in a power struggle. Quite the contrary. Like the professional prize fighter who, no matter how psychologically and emotionally abandoned, abused, impoverished and demoralized in his childhood, fights fiercely and unforgivingly once he steps into the ring, the inveterate power broker, to the discouragement of his adversaries or victims, generally proves to be a tougher and better competitor than they are.

By contrast, it is in the area of kindness, empathy and responsiveness to human needs that the person bent on the acquisition and enactment of power seems so bereft. And this is exactly what the recipient of a power transaction often intuitively senses: a chilling awareness of imposed isolation born of the recognition that the other with whom one is unhappily entangled seems to be operating from a psychical space in which the desire for intimate rapport simply does not matter.

THE EMPATHY OF EMPOWERMENT

Since we are considering everyday, non-sociopathic interpersonal situations that are practically universal, empathy, to a greater or lesser extent, must be present. With this difference: in a power transaction empathy is directed towards the anxiety that the other is perceived to be experiencing concerning issues over acquiring, maintaining or possibly losing power. Thus, someone in power (for example, a boss) may be genuinely empathic to how a subordinate is reacting to be instructed, criticized, dominated or, especially, ordered about. They may conduct corporate interpersonal seminars in order to discover a better strategy for dealing with what Goffman terms loss of face, but this loss of face will be vis-a-vis the imagined social perception of one's lack of deference. What such empathy will characteristically not reach to is that part of the true self that does not care about and is not caught up in conflicts over and resistances to power operations.

There is probably no more classic example of this than the stereotypical reaction of the boss who finds himself in the unpleasant position of having to fire a person who has been a loyal employee for a period of several years. There is then, usually, among other things: an unavoidable and fairly acute awareness of the mortification of the individual who is being discharged; a wish to offer partial immediate reparation by guiltily enumerating all the presumed accomplishments of the one who is being summary terminated; and the offer of the standard compensation in the form of severance pay and the willingness to provide a laudatory recommendation to prospective employers.

On the one hand, empathy is shown hereby by the attempt to temper the disappointment and cushion the shock of the other with patent blandishments, such as, "I don't really think we're right for you and that you'd be happy if you stayed." On the other hand, such empathy, if not pseudo, can often simultaneously be self-serving inasmuch as the boss generally has the ulterior motive of tranquillizing the terminated employee in order to forestall a public display of retaliative anger or protracted, ostentatious sulking that would disrupt the customary work flow, while proving distinctly embarrassing to the company and potentially damaging to morale.

For all of these reasons, almost never does the person let go feel any true nurturance was received. Instead, the empathy in evidence is geared to the other's sensitivity and responsiveness to a painful loss of face and deference. The person qua person, other than as a reactor to a disturbing shift in power, does not figure in the equation. There seems little discernible interest in what significance the event-- outside of the immediate dire consequences of loss of prestige, income and so on-- will hold in the mind of the person and in what way, for better or worse, their life course will now be altered. And, curiously, almost never is the event considered by the boss in the context of his present relationship with his ersatz employee. How does the manner, style, warmth or lack of it, and undeniable fact of the decision to terminate reflect on the history of the pair and what does it bode for the future?

It is in the nature of a blatant power operation, of course, for such interpersonal niceties to seem self-evidently irrelevant. And therein lies one of the sources of its ability to influence the other: by compelling him to think, primarily in terms of push and pull, levers and leverage, advantage and disadvantage, winner and loser, having face and losing face, so that when he does think of the relationship, he typically thinks of it resentfully, that is in terms of the politics of power, which is a far cry from envisioning it in all of its multi-dimensions (only one of which is power). It follows it is also in the nature of power, and part of the power of power, that once it has reared its ugly head and the subordinate other has been officially disempowered, the underlying relationship as such is therefore tarnished and almost never can it go back--especially in regard to the possibilities of intimacy--to what it was before.

One of the great difficulties, as already mentioned, in parent-child relations when it comes to instructing, educating, disciplining, punishing and ordering, is to be able to put the obvious and enormous power differential in brackets so as to infuse the necessary doses of reparative empathy and, accordingly, one of the reasons that so-called golden moments--when parent and child spontaneously, creatively, playfully take pleasure in one another's company--tend to be rare is that unresolved issues of power often tend to dominate.

As heir to this early familial difficulty, adult displays of empathy vis-á-vis power operations--especially those involving manifest inequities that are the product of discrepant role functioning--are too often limited to the understanding of the vicissitudes of power as they affect the self only in an immediate, worldly and pragmatic fashion (and not to the needs of the true self which are actually far more important at precisely this juncture).

USING

With some justice, the preferred mode of interpersonal relating of someone who is engaged in a power play could be called using. Unconsciously, the interaction as such is reified as a commodity, to be purchased at the lowest psychic cost. Competition, self-interest, the desire to encroach upon the other's territory are seen as merely by-products of an underlying entrepreneurial agenda. So it is worth noting what the desire to use the other as product leaves out: a reciprocal urge to be used in turn, a curiosity in whatever can be obtained from the other regardless of whether it has any immediate practical benefits, a belief that something tangible can be learned from the other, that the future of the transaction may be much more important than the prospects of the present. In other words, use of the other may be something sufficiently complex that it has to be deferred, approached on its own terms and allowed to evolve--that is, when it comes to interrelating as opposed to grasping and acquiring an object, one begins by building a foundation.

POWER GAMES

1.   Withholding Approval.

A simple power game that is disarmingly effective derives from the almost inexhaustible availability of opportunity for one person to tellingly withhold approval from another.

The preconditions for withholding approval are: a perception that the other will not be satisfied to just do whatever he is doing but requires a degree of validation from the person, which in turn implies that the person presumably knows how to discriminate and can be counted on to render a reasonably objective appraisal if he or she elects to do so. The other then completes what he set out to do and, after a certain amount of time has elapsed, along with some standard cues to the person for approbation, waits for a positive response. When approval is withheld in this common scenario for any of a number of reasons, a compelling dynamic can get played out.

Typically, the performer wonders if the person is critical of the performance but rather than say so, says nothing, hoping that the person perhaps may be lulled out of his or her judgmental frame of mind. Or he may conclude that his performance was so unremarkable that it actually passed by completely unnoticed. In either case, the performer is likely to feel rejected. Whatever self-esteem issues were meant to be ameliorated by the performance of the act, have only been aggravated, except now there does not appear to be any immediate relief in sight. Whatever hope there was for affirmation has more or less collapsed. More painfully self-conscious than before, he can only bide his time, go through the motions until he can get away and try to figure out what went wrong.

Each person knows on some level, both consciously and unconsciously, that every other person they encounter will require minimal affirmation: that they exist, that they are a human being, that they have a true self, a social self, a repertoire of specific attributes, qualities, skills, a history of experiences, and finally, that they are thereby a person entitled to certain rights to be validated by acts of deference (Goffman). And there is no one who will not be affected in some way if they perceive or imagine they perceive any other person who seems to be withholding any of these fundamental affirmations. Each of us therefore realizes they have the power to disturb the psychic equilibrium of anyone they meet--if they care--simply by failing to register the appropriate validation required by that person which, of course, will vary considerably from individual to individual.

It is worth noting that a good part of the necessary affirmation that is sought is--not so much because one needs to hear they possess minimal worth--but because they need to be reassured they are not going to suffer the trauma of encountering someone who will manifestly find their presence unbearably offensive. Although most people who are not grossly handicapped physically, socially, mentally or psychologically will be able to count on the majority of those whom they meet (out of a sense of a certain existential solidarity as well as the rules of civil social interaction) to accord them a modicum of credit for being fellow members of the human species, they will never be sure that a given individual may not be the exception who will despise them at first sight. It is just this interpersonal catastrophe, neither probable nor that uncommon, that people devoutly wish to avoid.

And the greatest reassurance--far more than any perfunctory run-through of the social amenities, which are designed to cover up rather than reveal honest feelings--will be an indication that the other has sensed and appropriately responded in some way or another to a real dimension of their true self. But this, of course, is what is so rarely seen, at least in any unambiguous fashion. In its stead, people are left to ponder how what has been said and done secretly reflects what each of them thinks and feels, doesn't think or feel, values or devalues, and likes or dislikes about the other. Ironically, not only can validation of what could be called the social self be an obstacle to the search for such meaningful interpersonal signs, but if misused (and it often is), it can become a source of active invalidation of the true self: this is because there is a hunger for intimacy and recognition of the significance of the true self that, when enough time has lapsed, will no longer be satisfied with the simple stroking of the social self--the unconscious attempt to restrict the relationship to the level of only a banal exchange of meaningless pleasantries.

But there's the rub: affirmation of the true self--unlike that of the social self where one can rightfully protest infractions of interpersonal protocol (acting in an insensitive, indifferent, or insulting fashion, showing insufficient deference and so on)--cannot be solicited. It is instead to be freely given and it is considered beneath a person's dignity to point out that he or she requires to be more genuinely liked, loved or esteemed. (By contrast, as shown by Goffman, 1967, there is a well-established repertory of social protocol allowing the person to vigorously contest instances of unjust social degradation and violations of the so-called civil rights of the self). It follows that the person who is in the position of withholding approval may feel that he has an ace up his sleeve, with all attention being focused on the mini, psychic soap opera of whether he is going to come through and reward the performance that is tacitly being played out (all of which allows deeper issues of the self pertaining to intimacy to be safely ignored or sensibly postponed).

For all of these reasons, each of us has the potential--simply by withholding approval, especially of the self--to thereby almost endlessly tantalize the other. And when the one who is withholding validation is someone who is intent upon playing a power game, the message often becomes: only when my transaction is satisfactorily completed, will approval be given. Put another way, approval is meted out according to how well the other facilitates the person's wish for empowerment. Approval in this instance is for the act, the performance, the result, denouément and the aftermath. It is never prior, never for the process alone and never on behalf of the self.

2.	Interpersonal Relativity Theory or "That's Your Opinion"

There is a huge difference between acknowledging that--while viewpoints are subjectively informed--there may be common grounds for integrating differences, and the idea that relativity subverts the authority of any one perspective and that even the deepest perspective based on the widest array of digested life experience is just an opinion! This, of course, is the ethos of egalitarianism applied litigiously to the interpersonal realm. To assert dogmatically that every idea is equal is to politicize both thinking and the psyche. Someone insisting on psychical relativity, therefore, is really making a political rather than a substantive, veridical statement: i.e., what essentially matters is not truth as such, but the right of the psyche to vote.

By saying "that's your opinion"--in other words, I have as much a right to express myself as you do--one unconsciously subverts what is often a potentially meaningful incongruity or misalliance of selves into a pseudo political issue that in turn typically becomes an interpersonal blind alley.

3.   Use of Pain

The great psychoanalyst, W.R. Bion (1992), considered the capacity to bear the pain of development, which in his view entailed the bringing together of the primitive and the sophisticated parts of the psyche, to be an intrinsic feature of healthy growth and a milestone of maturity. By contrast, the power player has a different use for psychic pain: he may wonder how much of it the other can endure and to that end calibrate the amount of pressure to be applied. The unconscious assumption then is that if the inequity of power is sufficient, it cannot be withstood (in other words, when it comes to pain, everyone has their price). From such a perspective it follows if the other is being uncommonly resistant that either the imbalance in leverage has been inadequately demonstrated or inadequately applied.

It is a characteristic of the power player, therefore, that he cannot believe that a substantial differential in psychic force can be surmounted or safely absorbed. For him the only possible answer--since he believes winning is everything and no one can be satisfied with losing--is the marshalling of more power. For the power player, pain arises either when one has too little leverage or as an immediate response to the direct impact of someone else's greater power. From this vantage point, pain is regarded as a reaction to a loss of power and not to the loss of love, of intimacy or of a relationship. It is the stunned reaction to a forceful blow rather than the symptom of impoverishment, lack of nurturance, nourishment or the sign of a void in the self.

There is a sense, therefore, in which power can be perceived as an antidote to pain, and the more one is in pain, the greater will be the need for power. But to acknowledge that one is in pain--analogous to the loss of face experienced by the depressive upon recognition that he or she feels unloved--is to acknowledge a weakness and not surprisingly this is often displaced by the less shameful awareness that one is merely thirsting for power.

The relationships that each person has to his or her pain can therefore be conceived of as a distinctive object relation. Pain, for example, can unconsciously be regarded as the psychic equivalent of illness, something which symptomatically points to a concealed, unhealthy locus. It can be experienced as a mysterious inner rallying force which polarizes all those parts of the self not in pain versus those which unfortunately are. To the degree that it can thereby quickly organize self experience, it can make sense of what might otherwise seem ambivalent and chaotic. By creating the immediate goal of intrapsychically uniting against a common enemy, pain provides instant meaning. Someone in real pain, for example, does not doubt what he wants to do--primarily to relieve the pain--although he may be quite discouraged as to how and where to begin.

The endurance of pain is often taken as a badge of red courage. To the extent that one is suffering but has not submitted to one's suffering, there is evidence of courage. Pain can then be interpreted to the self as proof that one is alive--not numb and deadened. Indeed, since no feeling is more vivid than pain--so long as one can feel that--one cannot be dead. In addition, pain can also be proof that one cares. Since most psychic pain concerns loss of some kind, pain shows one is not indifferent, cynical or unconnected to what happens.

Finally, pain can be confirmation that one is interesting, a romantic who perhaps has a touch of the suffering poet in him, with depths or a soul, if you will. It can thereby be a sign that one's life is after all dramatic and not humdrum and boring; that one is not insensate, not something finished but a person in flux. It can be a reminder that one has an inside, is not a machine and can serve as an evocative warning to anyone within earshot, "Be careful. I can be fragile, too."

More importantly, it can be a signal that someone is not okay, and may be in need of attention, of being helped or loved. It can even be an ironic symbol of hope--inasmuch as really severe pain can seem unbearable--that change (and the motivation to make change happen) must be in the offing and to that extent, it can unconsciously indicate that something dreadful is coming to an end or to a head.

Above all, perhaps, pain is a plea that a person should be judged by their vulnerability and not just their strength. But it is obvious, the power player disregards most of these meanings of pain. Instead, he or she is content basically to gauge how well the other can withstand pain by trying to appraise how they will respond to pressure, manipulation, intimidation and so on. Even more tellingly, they do not see it as relevant to assess the amount of frustration and subsequent resistance which the concomitant suppression of the other's true self will engender.

4.   The Betrayal of Trust

One of the things a therapist is privy to are the acts of betrayal, to which we are all vulnerable. Someone confesses to their lover that they have never really loved them; tells their friend that they no longer respect them; confronts their parent with the bitter recrimination that they believe they have been given very little in life. To say or do something profoundly wounding such as this is to immediately put into disarray an other who now can do little but mobilize their defenses. Savagely going on the offensive, therefore, is to ensure that basic trust is impossible. By creating an interpersonal drama based on deeply hurt feelings, a scenario is established--where two people can no longer come together--but which seems poignant and meaningful enough to perpetuate. Because they are so vivid, the pain and sense of betrayal make it easy to overlook the fact that the new inner, usually secret relationship that has been fashioned is comparatively lifeless and static.

One of the remarkable aspects about such grudge-like object relations is how much they seem to give the self while not giving at all. By continually reenacting the original scenario of abandonment, they simultaneously stimulate and elicit lively revenge fantasies. But they go nowhere. Unconsciously, the sense that reparation is impossible because irreparable harm has been done--that therefore appropriate retaliation, in order to be commensurate to the enormous unjust deprivation incurred, would have to be frighteningly and perhaps uncontrollably global in its destructiveness--make it seem necessary to seal off and internalize any honest expression of feeling. It is thereby repetitive and even obsessive without seeming so.

The violation of what Erik Erikson (1951) has famously called a basic sense of trust--the inculcated childhood belief that one is entitled to expect to be dealt with fairly--adds the weight of family tradition to the injured party's indignation. It follows the matter is further compounded, when the act of betrayal is perceived as a direct consequence of an advantage in power enjoyed by the perpetrator (e.g., such as a boss). Unconsciously, the complaint that is lodged is that anything short of the empathic use of one's authority is unfair. The instances of unempathic hierarchical power that permeate our social landscape--in spite of their insistence, as mentioned, that they are built on meritorious achievement and not a thirst to lord it over subordinates--in this way run deeply counter to our familial expectation of fair treatment and to that extent seem a betrayal of basic trust.

Thus, an underling, an employee, or anyone who feels abused in a relationship in which the other is perceived, for any reason whatsoever, as holding the reins, almost insidiously gets hooked on the power inequities, unfairness and the drama of injustice; in short, on everything which is depriving about being subjected in reality or imagination to a transaction based on power. Imperceptibly, the complexity of the relationship becomes overshadowed by the internal lamentation over the hurt one has received, while simultaneously the often theatrical quality of betrayal of basic trust--creating a kind of soap opera of the self--can provide a pseudo reparation for the sense of underlying, obsessive deprivation of the one who feels betrayed.

5.   Being Mad

Closely linked to the sense of betrayal is the feeling of entitled, the investment in holding onto and being mad at someone who is perceived to have wronged you. The person who is being mad may then variously experience himself as appearing dynamic, proud, impressively well-defended, independent-minded, dangerous to be around, showing heart, and not only taking himself and any injustice done to him quite seriously but capable of reacting with courage--all of which contributes to a sense that something is building towards a possibly interesting change (the aggressive counterpart to the uses and meanings of pain).

Typically, being mad is abetted by the unconscious wish to keep on feeling that way, as opposed to impulsive anger where the drive is for immediate discharge. Being mad can therefore be conceived as a kind of coy, withholding or exhibitionistic anger. Such a person may want to punish the other with rejecting feelings rather than with a concrete action, or deliver what is intended as emotional blackmail: a plain threat of what might happen but hasn't happened yet, unless some appropriate reparation is made (in contrast to the expression of punitive anger which is analogous to a sentence being passed and is meant to be a deterrence against a repetition of the original offense).

It follows there can be something unpleasantly mesmerizing about witnessing and experiencing another person who is mad at you. The other may then seem to have their finger figuratively on the trigger, to be poised on the edge of a psychical diving board, to be in a state of precarious knife-point balance, their emotion like a pulsating, coiled spring: as though they are about to reach the end of their tether, are nearing their threshold of volatile discharge, where the slightest adverse pressure might push them past the point of no return.

Although obvious, it is worth noting that being mad creates an atmosphere of interpersonal suspense. Sooner or later the emotion, unless it abates, will become too intense to be sustained, and this will be true even for someone who can hold onto their grudge-like anger for years. Characteristically, the times when it is actively displayed or revived are comparatively rare--because anger by its nature is a self-immolating emotion which, once it has sufficiently primed itself and reached its peak, will instinctively seek discharge or down time.

The other, who unconsciously knows this, therefore waits and wonders not only when it will be over but what is going to happen thereafter. There is an intuitive understanding that someone who stops being mad thereby creates an emotional and interpersonal discontinuity--with no real transition existing from being visibly angry to becoming more safely civil--that typically will inaugurate a moratorium of sorts. This is the time when the other may try to muddle his way back and retrieve what can be retrieved of the prior, pre-anger relationship, while simultaneously recognizing that the relationship as such--even if the show of anger has been comparatively minor--has perhaps been permanently changed. All of which means that added interpersonal investment may be required in the future.

So long, however, as the person continues to be demonstrably mad, the other must brace himself or herself, putting the true self on hold. And therein lies its power. Someone who is actively being mad is tantamount to being in fifth gear when it comes to their normal level of aggression. Unconsciously they know--due to their adrenalin rush--that they probably have access to more combative energy than at almost any other time and, because of this, they are likely to be feared.

6.   "You Have To Answer For Santino"

In those famously chilling words, which occur towards the end of The Godfather, Michael Corleone tells his instantly-terrified brother-in-law that he is about to be held accountable for having fingered Santino to be assassinated.

When it is the psychopathic version of holding someone to account that is being depicted--as portrayed in gangster movies such as The Godfather--closure usually does not arrive until sometime after the guilty party has been murdered. This example, just because it is so extreme, shows clearly what can be so intimidating about the enactment of accountability:

Perhaps foremost is that issues of relating do not enter into it. Whatever happens to the culprit--their fate--will depend instead on the application of a comparatively abstract principle or rule of behavior. When the criterion that matters is a pragmatic one of consequences and not the quality of one's actions, the other who is being put on the carpet, in effect, is being accused of a kind of behavioral negligence (or malpractice if it is professional ineptitude that is being singled out).

Now this, of course, is in contrast to ordinary interrelating where there is an unconscious and reciprocal sense that at any moment either party may have just engendered a narcissistic injury in the other and, if necessary, a concomitant evaluation of a range of options for making reparation (before it may ever reach consciousness in the form of a wish to make the other responsible). It is worth noting, however, when accountability is the issue, it is only one person who is being held accountable and only one person who is exacting it.

It becomes immediately apparent that what making the other accountable for their actions does is to thereby stop the forward thrust of the relationship--like calling a moratorium until the alleged injurious past behavior has been dealt with. Analogous to the reaction to a perceived criminal act, all bets are off; the regular perks and privileges that go along with everyday interrelating are rescinded until the pattern of offensive behavior has been satisfactorily rectified.

The point is that this is scary. What normally is either not dealt with or relegated to unconscious communication, is now being held up to a potentially ongoing public scrutiny. It follows that almost automatically the opportunities for spontaneous and playful interacting are annulled as behavior is now looked at from an essentially moralistic framework. From the standpoint of intimacy, therefore, trying to make the other interpersonally accountable is a non-reciprocal, hierarchical transaction of often punitive intent.

The typical response of the person being held accountable is initial shock at how seriously the other is taking behavior that just moments ago seemed to have been acceptable, often followed by an attempt to defuse whatever accusations are being made with a show of propitiating behavior--perhaps a gently scolding or disclaiming smile as though to say, "Oh come on". If the attribution of misconduct is not forthwith recanted, various defenses will come into play: an exaggerated display of how surprised one is, meant to thereby disown agency (even if the objectionable behavior in question did happen, it was purely unintentional); angry indignation; outright denial; counterattack; and projective identification (no, it is you who are being offensive to me).

The most general defense strategy will be to attenuate the new tone of moral gravity by reminding the aggrieved party of all those past aspects of the relationship currently under fire that speak against the allegations of misconduct and to thereby suggest a more benign interpretation of the objectionable behavior in question. In the sense that here the intent plainly is to recontextualize an experience which has been injuriously received by the other, we can speak of the unfolding of a psychic, interpersonal equivalent of a criminal trial: a process wherein for every accusatory statement that is presented, a defense of some sort will be thrown up.

Such relatively simple resistance can be surprisingly effective. It is often overlooked that even a defensive posture that is ineffectual from the standpoint of raising cogent counter arguments is still powerful to the extent that it delivers the message that the person has abandoned all hope of collaborating and is instead intent on channelling all available energies towards an oppositional stance (to make this point even clearer, think of how much of the rules and etiquette of social interaction are there to prevent one or the other from abruptly giving up on the tacit goal of interpersonal compatibility in order to retreat into a manifestly defensive mode). It is obvious this kind of armored presentation of the self will be unsettling to the other if only because it indicates that added work will now be necessary to deal with it. (Perhaps this is most classically illustrated in the characteristically tortured and protracted nature of the criminal trial where so much is riding on the outcome-- literally life, liberty and the pursuit of happiness--of the adversarial relationship of the parties.)

It is worth noting that intimacy, by contrast, will often try to constructively confront whatever psychic truth there may be in the reprimand of one's partner and even to collaboratively revisit it in the service of working on the relationship.

It follows someone who is being held accountable will have no such luxury. Mistrust, coupled with active defensiveness, will govern the transaction as each party will tend to seek an advantage and leverage over the other. Sooner or later there will be a near exclusive reliance on strategy, game playing, one-upmanship, winning and losing, attacking and defending. This is the stuff, of course, of power games which therefore will go hand in hand with the need to hold someone accountable, the performance-based perspective of the power-imbued state of mind lending itself irresistibly to such transactions. And the gross lack of relating will be rationalized by such standbys as hierarchical nurturance: e.g., "This is for your own good"; or, "You'll thank me for this one day"; or, "I am entitled to do this".

Not surprisingly, the dynamics of adult accountability will in large measure be a derivative of parent-child interactions as internalized in ego-superego relations. If, as shown, parental transactions aimed at eliciting accountability from their children are so rarely empathically enacted, and if the pervasive social sanctions designed to enforce proper respect for such standard authority figures as an employer, a teacher, a police officer, professional or anyone else in good social standing are even more strikingly devoid of empathy for the putative offender--it is easy to see, in such instances, how an almost knee-jerk, transferential sense of being unfairly deprived will develop.

And perhaps nowhere will this be more clearly in evidence than in the relationship of our own ego to our own superego. Again, if we assume that the parental prohibitions and admonitions from which the nucleus of the infantile conscience was formed were characteristically harshly administered (bullying the child being the modus operandi) and that the parental role model for behavior considered praiseworthy from which the nucleus of the ego ideal was formed was typically enacted in a pressuring way--it is no wonder we are so vulnerable to interpersonal reprimanding. To find the root of this susceptibility, we have only to look at the ordinary dynamics of a commonplace conflict between ego and superego.

It is characteristic of such an inner conflict whenever we think we are letting ourselves or others down, that on the one hand we believe we are behaving badly and inexcusably in our own eyes, while on the other hand we are certain we can and should do better. Typically we then imagine what we should have done and wished we had done. Walter Mitty fantasies of heroic self-vindication, however, tend to provide scant comfort as sooner or later we return to a sober consideration of what others who witnessed or will hear about our distinctly less than worthy presentation of ourself are likely to now think of us. Perhaps then in an effort to recover we may console ourselves with all the possible extenuating circumstances of our imagined recent disgrace, dredge up all the countering favorable aspects of our past performance--psychic character witnesses called to our defense--and map plausible, reassuring strategies for damage control in the future.

Note that in all of this the conscience stays disapprovingly silent and the ego ideal, meant to inspire us, seems even more inaccessible than before. It is significant to me, therefore, not only how remarkably little nurturance is afforded in such everyday crises of self esteem by our conscience and ego ideal--that rather than dynamically interacting with our self, impose themselves as more or less structurally frozen, indifferent and forbidding presences--but how ready we are to accept such intrapsychic deprivation. For how rare it is when we feel that our conscience, instead of judging us, likes us and that our ego ideal, instead of frustrating us with its aloofness, actively encourages and even cares about us. Ironically, the parts of the psyche that nurture the self (what Bollas, 1987, has called subject relations) do not seem to come from the conscience and ego ideal. This is another way of saying, of course, that in general ego-superego relations tend to be profoundly non-reciprocal and hierarchical. In one important sense they thereby are an intrapsychic guarantor of our vulnerability to worldly, interpersonal power plays. (As Freud, 1923, noted, it as though the oedipal laying down of the superego simultaneously creates a permanent weakness in the ego in its relations to the new internalized structure.)

It follows that power operations, more often than not, will dominate the relations between the ego and superego. And here is a primary intrapsychic root cause of why it can seem so natural and irresistibly right-minded to fall into, buy into, invest in, resist or pursue what we have been describing as power plays and games. (It is obvious the relations of our ego to our unconscious, as illustrated in the paradigmatic defense mechanism of repression--conceptualized by Freud along lines of domination, patriarchy and banishment (as Christopher Bollas has ingeniously pointed out)--entail power operations on an even grander scale, but this is not the place to go into that.

In the next chapter we will explore the impact of power games in the one domain in which theoretically they are not supposed to flourish: therapy.

CHAPTER FOUR
Therapy Games

When it works, therapy is supposed to be built on trust, collaboration, and the making of a new kind of therapeutic relationship leading to greater insight and a broader perspective. Perhaps even more important--for promoting the necessary trust--than the esteem in which the patient holds the therapist (the positive transference) is what has been called the real relationship. Closer to what is commonly meant by the term 'therapeutic personality', the real relationship will have little to do with professional technique as such and will be based instead on what is perceived as being really there and, especially, as worthy of being trusted. But what, of course, will stand in the way of the genuinely trustworthy real relationship being established--upon which, with the help of legitimate technique a therapeutic relationship can be facilitated--is the formidable hierarchical, non-reciprocal structure of the artificial therapeutic situation. According to the theme of this book, that is from the standpoint of power, we now examine the respective roles of patient and therapist.

THE DIFFERENCE OF POWER

The Patient

The patient has been variously identified as someone who is alternately sick, dysfunctional, demoralized, needy, requiring outside professional help, confused and in general unable to manage on one's own. It is presumed that part of what is wrong with the patient is that he does not know what is wrong with him. He is ignorant of what he most needs to understand. Furthermore, there is a consensus that whatever is wrong probably has been that way, even if present in only a latent form, for a very long time. The patient therefore is in need of specialized knowledge, specialized help and new tools to better survive in the world. This tendency to think of therapy as an important commodity distributed by the mental health profession that is being put out on the market, reinforces such a perspective.

Perhaps the greatest inequity is the non-reciprocal nature of the therapeutic situation. The patient is expected to express himself more candidly than he has ever before to a professional stranger who is both trained and obligated by the ethics of his or her profession to be emotionally and psychologically neutral. The patient cannot question or explore, except in the most superficial manner, the private life and psyche of the therapist. He must take on faith--since he is ignorant of the process of technique and therefore unequipped to judge when it is working and when it is not--that there is value to the investment he is making. He cannot rely on credentials, because credentials refer, not to the individual ability of the person before him which is all that really matters, but an arbitrary and abstract level of training. He cannot rely on immediate feedback as he can with a doctor or surgeon because, unless the therapy, by design, is exceedingly short term, promising almost immediate benefits--and traditional mainstream psychotherapy as a rule is careful to avoid promising quick relief--he can anticipate at best, a deferred payoff.

The Therapist

By contrast, the therapist is presumably a comparatively successful, functioning professional, someone who has been mentally tried, tested and is currently well put together, with no outstanding personal problems that would stand in the way of concentrating his full attention on the patient before him. It follows such a therapist knows who he or she is, lives a life that is meaningful, is a member in good standing in his or her community and so on. Perhaps the enormous difference in power between them can be made clearer if we now consider their respective positions from the standpoint of social prestige and especially, in the light of expectations of performance.

Thus, it is noteworthy that for the prospective patient--short of showing up for the session for which he has contracted, being non-violent when he arrives and, eventually, sooner rather than later, paying for services rendered--almost nothing is expected. In other words, it is a staple of professional training that the therapist is schooled to be unblanchingly accepting of whatever may be the social status of the person who happens to walk through the door. Which means, providing that person treats the therapist in a non-violent manner and seems capable of paying for his sessions, he can also be recently released from jail, a closed psychiatric ward or outlandishly and inappropriately dressed (e.g., in a bathing suit and sandals, although cannot be naked), coming down from an horrific drug binge, presently in a confused state, deranged, actively hallucinating, someone who has just been abused, victimized, traumatized, publicly humiliated, fired from his or her job, abandoned in a relationship, who may be barely literate, subsisting on welfare, with a history of having been profoundly anti-social for many years.

Now let's look again by contrast, at the expectations which the prospective patient is typically encouraged to entertain regarding the social status and prestige of the professional he or she is preparing to meet. Such a therapist must be appropriately attired (thus, even an unremoved, visible soup stain on an otherwise clean shirt might raise a justifiable eyebrow), well groomed (if, for example, the therapist happens to be a man who is conspicuously unshaven, something is terribly wrong), in command of all the basic social amenities (behavior in the slightest bit odd is not to be tolerated: e.g., whistling or humming a tune while shaking the hand of the new arriving patient would immediately mark him as incompetent); equipped with the vocabulary and articulation of someone who is clearly better educated than the average (and cannot thereby idly employ off-color expressions, slang, crack jokes, relate anecdotes); in control of his emotions at all times, even in situations of extreme stress (if, for example, just minutes prior to the beginning of a scheduled session, the therapist has learned of a serious illness in his immediate family he is not expected to discuss, reveal it in any way or even allow it to internally distract him from the primary work at hand).

Furthermore, as part of his professionalism the therapist is required to tolerate whatever personal attacks, cheap shots, character assassination and ridicule come his way not only without responding in kind, but while continuing to empathize with the patient's point of view in an effort to facilitate the progress of his or her treatment. The therapist is somehow supposed to have bodily urges such as hunger or the need to go to the bathroom sufficiently in check so that--short of an emergency--he will not give in to them in the course of an ongoing session. And it is therefore not uncommon for patients who have been in therapy for years to be able to honestly say that they have never once observed their therapist take a bite out of a single morsel of food, excuse themselves to go to the bathroom, express frank disapproval, criticize them, lose their temper, become clearly frustrated or raise their voice above a certain professionally decorous level of expression.

We have, thus, on the one hand, a patient who is permitted, if not expected, to be dysfunctional, perhaps deranged, in an almost infinite variety of ways short of hurting himself or herself so as to require hospitalization; and, on the other hand, a therapist who, if he carried out his regular life according to the same code of conduct he adheres to in his office, would be someone who was much closer to a saint than to the basically secular middle class mental health professional he typically is.

It seems obvious to me that these intrinsic inequities of the non-reciprocal therapeutic situation make it a fertile soil for the proliferation of power games for whoever wants or needs to use them. Although there are no doubt hundreds of such games (to be depicted in a future book), what follows are just a few of the more important ones.

GAMES THERAPISTS PLAY

I begin with the therapist, first, not because I think they are more game-playing than patients but because--due to the weight of their authority and responsibility they carry--such untherapeutic behavior cannot help but have serious consequences for the progress of the treatment. Also, it is easier to overlook their game-playing because it tends to be shielded by their status as expert while being less conspicuously acted out than those of their patients.

1.   Meeting Socrates

There are few roles in our society and almost certainly no opportunity afforded the average middle class mental health professional for impressing those he may encounter as being a deep thinker as well as a profound student of human nature who happens to be in possession of a saint-like character compared to what will be available in his routine functioning as a therapist. Just consider the enormous built-in temptations that lie at hand for donning the mantle of wisdom:

The therapist, for openers, is by far the most mysterious and inaccessible person with whom the patient has ever had a relationship. The most august religious personage--even the holder of the highest political office in the land--will not enjoy the privilege of withholding basic autobiographical data to the same extent. What's more, such lack of disclosure is to be understood--far from being the product of an inability to relate--as a sign that the therapist is prepared to almost completely efface the fundamental expression of his own true self in order to facilitate the deepest possible exploration of the other.

While the therapist, of course, does not act as though he is privy to the answer, neither does he expatiate on what he does not know. It is therefore instructive to look at some of the things the therapist chooses not to touch upon: while he customarily reveals numerous reservations, if not frank doubts, as to the cogency of many of the patient's remarks and thought processes, he rarely shares a lack of trust in the essential soundness of his own psychic apparatus (and the more he may be doubting it, the less likely is he to share it); he almost never discloses the lacunae in his formal training, the particular areas he feels he needs to grow in, the difficulty in grasping or applying certain subtleties of theory or clinical practice and so on. Not only does he completely delete from therapy the dimensions of his ignorance of psychic reality in general and of the patient in particular, but he often fosters the impression they do not exist (here Adam Phillips', 1996, shrewd observation is apt that it is hard for psychoanalysts not to include into their theory a theory of the unknown).

Put another way, we could say that often psychoanalysts and psychodynamically-oriented therapists seem to want it both ways: they want credit for what they know and credit for what they do not know. This, of course, is a misuse and caricature of the founder of psychoanalysis who in actuality was at his best when he was trying to infer, sense, intuit and hypothesize vis-á-vis the boundaries and functions of the unconscious. In my view, therefore, the famous chapter seven of The Interpretation of Dreams (1900)--where Freud lays out the dynamics of the unconscious mind, based on his exhaustive studies of the formation of dreams--is the crowning achievement of his vast oeuvre. What a far cry that is from the present trendy and almost obligatory usage of the word unconscious--as though to call a psychic process unconscious and to say nothing more than that is to say something profound. And again, by contrast, how different from such mundane, pretentious dabbling in the unknown is the project of a great contemporary psychoanalyst such as Christopher Bollas who strives mightily to come to grips with and broaden our understanding of the work of unconscious experience in pathbreaking books like The Shadow of the Object (1987), Being a Character (1993) and Cracking Up (1995).

For all of these reasons, it can become deceptively easy for the workaday psychotherapist to become enamored with silence, mystery, pregnant pauses and an accompanying classic blank screen persona meant to signal transcendent objectivity. Whatever such a therapist then communicates may be duly offered as at the very least speculative knowledge of the self he seems to be so intently observing. Even his perplexment, his rank ignorance, shrouded as it is in enigma, more often than not, can pass for thoughtfulness or perhaps wisdom. His asceticism, the fact that he assiduously refrains from giving into the press of ordinary bodily, emotional or sexual needs while immersed in his work, combined with his interpersonal stoicism--his refusal to voice protest, fight back or even mildly defend himself regardless of how maligned or unjustly provoked--can create an aura of saintliness. Although quite understandable from the vantage point of the patient, it is decidedly less so and even deleterious once the therapist--as, unfortunately, frequently happens--begins to believe and use his ready-made clinical press clippings to manipulate the therapeutic situation for his personal advantage.

2.   Putting The Patient In Her Place

In everyday life, it is considered rude not to respond to someone who addresses you, while protracted silence is taken as frank hostility. Not so in therapy, where silence, at least theoretically, can be used to facilitate: a listening space that is free of conversational distractions; a more receptive medium for the elaboration of meaning; the purchase of additional time--by deferring the customary response--in which to process unconscious experience (necessitated in part by the kind of free-associative, playful discourse especially encouraged by psychoanalytic therapy which is not meant to be crammed into functionally cohesive, narrative sound bites).

Now the point is, because of this built-in rationale, it becomes easy and tempting for the therapist who happens to be angry to frustrate his patient by refusing to speak. Thus, the therapist (as Racker, 1968, has noted) can punish the patient with silence. In addition, the therapist who has a countertransferential need to do so, can unsettle the patient simply by remaining emotionally neutral--that is, by covertly identifying with all of the negative connotations of his decision not to express his true self. After all, much of the power of the ordinary withholding personality derives from an analogous perplexity that is engendered in the mind of the other: to wit, is the person not expressing himself because what he is thinking and feeling is too unpleasant, critical or threatening, or because he has yet to be sufficiently stimulated by the other into investing in a reaction of some kind or is it because the person is merely waiting for a more opportune time to speak his mind? To gain satisfaction by frustrating the other with silence and the withholding of any discernible emotional warmth are two ways by which a therapist who may be afraid of closeness can create distance and keep his needy patient at bay. A third, insidious way, is to simply stop viewing the patient as a therapeutic person as he is trained to do and instead begin to regard her as a social being (and thereby open the door to a host of subjectively-toned, potentially deprecating value judgments).

And, finally, the therapist can directly and interpersonally put the patient in her place by beginning to subtly, or not so subtly, identify with and simultaneously exude the aura of power and authority that goes hand in hand with the status of expert. The unconscious intention then is to remind the patient in case she needs it that she is in one way or another in a subordinate position to the therapist.

GAMES PATIENTS PLAY

"I'm From Missouri--Show Me"

The patient intuitively senses that psychotherapy at best is a soft science, that cannot be meaningfully quantified and certainly not rigorously replicated. She can therefore use this knowledge to make the therapist feel defensive--thereby successfully driving him out of his adopted stance of neutrality--and try to justify the value of his services. She knows the therapist, unless a specialist in brief therapy or behavior modification, cannot point to immediate benefits and on some level must be intimidated, as she is, by the awareness that ours is the age of the information superhighway, of Internet, web sites, and global communication where fact is god.

It follows all the patient has to do, to rattle even the most self-assured, veteran psychotherapist, is to embrace a cordial posture of skeptical curiosity. After all, she has a right as a consumer, who is being asked to pay a fixed sum of money on a regular basis, to inquire as to the precise nature of the service she is purchasing, the benefits that are being promised and the status of verifiability of the claims of help being made. Now it is a relatively simple matter for the therapist to supply--to the patient who is nervous about meeting him for the first time and inquires about his background and experience--a brief resume of his credentials, his training and career as a mental health professional.

It is an entirely different matter, however, to pretend to be able to verify the benefits he is hoping to offer the prospective patient. The therapist realizes, even in the best case scenario, the benefits to be derived from the process of psychotherapy are uncertain and deferred. If he is a very good therapist he may have confidence that if all goes well he will have an excellent chance of improving the patient's life situation, but he cannot know beforehand--so many psychical variables being at play--what are the odds that all actually will go well, which is really what the patient is asking. Such a prediction is most reliably made vis-á-vis a thing and not a person, and when it is made in regard to a person--as, for example, when psychiatrists discuss with a patient the ratio of cost versus benefits concerning a proposed psychotropic drug--it is invariably done so in reference to a comparatively isolated biochemical or behavioral component, and never to the complexity of a fundamentally unique life problem (which usually is why the patient is coming to therapy).

For all of these reasons, the patient who seeks power in the therapeutic situation can scarce do better than play the skeptic with her therapist.

"I Want A New Contract"

The standard contract in psychotherapy--that the patient is responsible for coming at a specified time, paying an agreed-upon fee and is invited and encouraged to be as utterly candid as is humanly possible with a guarantee of complete confidentiality from an experienced professional typically committed to a stance of neutrality and objectivity--is a reflection in part, as mentioned, of the non-reciprocal nature, the power differential and the inequity of the therapeutic situation. Nothing is therefore easier and more tempting for the person who is beginning therapy, who characteristically is anxious, mistrustful, cynical, discouraged and can find little reason to believe that substantive nurturance will be received from the other--than to wonder for whose benefit does this standard therapeutic contract exist? And from such innocent initial misgivings, it is a short step to convince oneself that it might be better to (if not rewrite) at least negotiate the contract that has been offered.

In spite of the fact this is what often happens, it is exceedingly difficult to forthrightly challenge a therapeutic contract. This is because, on the one hand, the patient is understandably intimidated regarding her grasp of the technical and professional basis for the contract, but on the other hand senses that the contract as such is supposedly based on universal ethical human conduct and to that extent within her ken. Furthermore, since she is going to be so deeply implicated in the immediate and long-term consequences of the therapeutic contract, she naturally feels it is not only her right but her duty to register whatever protest she has (analogous to the patient's right to hold their doctor accountable to a code of conduct deemed consonant with medical ethics).

A common strategy of the patient who mistrusts the therapeutic contract will be to bide her time while she waits for clearcut instances of her therapist being unprofessional: losing his temper, not paying attention, going to sleep, overcharging, cheating on the time, being judgmental, seductive, overtly punitive or perhaps considerably more inflexible in their makeup policy than that of another therapist one happens to hear of from a friend, and so on. The patient in effect secretly waits for examples of what she might consider therapeutic malpractice--a direct aftermath of the fact that the typical therapeutic setting does not allow for a fluid and reciprocal dialogue regarding contractual differences to take place. (In spite of the tradition among psychodynamically oriented psychotherapists to encourage their patients to freely express their negative transferential feelings towards their therapist's policy, it is a fact that patients for a variety of reasons rarely can avail themselves of this opportunity, short of transferentially acting it out.) What this means is that the patient tends to introduce a discussion of the therapeutic contract only after she believes she has been abused by it. Since therapists are unconsciously aware of this--even though they have been trained to be receptive to such resistive reservations--they are often countertransferentially wary of encountering them. It follows, when they do come up, there is typically a strained atmosphere during which the therapist, more often than not, to some extent, will unconsciously endeavor to sell the benefits of his particular style of practice.

Not surprisingly, the patient who perceives, as is likely to be the case, that her therapist has difficulty in discussing his policy without becoming defensive will also realize she has acquired a new weapon for driving her therapist out of his customary stance of neutrality. Thereafter--to the extent the patient feels narcissistically abused and needs to aggressively restore herself--much of her resistance to the acceptance of her therapist's individual policy regarding the fee, scheduling, requirements for makeups and so on will represent the exercise of a power operation rather than an honest attempt to express one's feelings vis-á-vis the particular arrangements of the therapeutic setting.

Such a patient will probably enjoy no greater power than to challenge the so-called therapeutic contract: for a key element of the contract will concern the fee to be paid for the services rendered and, more importantly, the right of the patient to decide whether or not to continue to employ the therapist. So far as the therapist is concerned, therefore--on a critical, practical and economic survival level--the patient who is articulating serious doubts as to the acceptability of the therapeutic contract, is simultaneously raising the possibility of firing the therapist. And whenever this issue is brought up, patient and therapist being human--all too human it is almost impossible for the specter of power and its vicissitudes not to creep over, if not dominate, the interaction.

3.   Not Relating.

The possibilities for not relating, or relationally hiding in therapy, are immense for both therapist and patient.

The patient, for example, has only to lose herself in the artificial world of the therapeutic setting without really investing in it: that is, to pretend to be wrestling with her defenses, to be lapsing into silence as she explores and processes a new type of free associative, unconscious communication, to be, all the while, gradually becoming a therapeutic person--as opposed to someone who really wants to withdraw and defer any genuine recognition of interpersonal difficulties, in particular, the wish not to relate.

As for the therapist, it is sometimes overlooked that before you can analyze a relationship, you have to have one. When technique is unconsciously enacted and perceived as what I have termed narcissistic giving--the belief that, somehow, merely by practicing a particular recommended technique, and presumably knowing how to do it, you were thereby benefiting a patient--then insidiously it is regarded as a substitute for relating. There arises then a shared illusion that the therapist who exercises and personifies a preferred technique and the patient who responds or resists responding to such clinical role-playing are somehow thereby relating, that they are working out a therapeutic relationship of a special kind--one that can be subsequently analyzed.

By contrast, I suggest that the therapeutic relationship as such doesn't actually begin until the participants authentically begin to relate in an at least partially intimate fashion. In other words--especially on the patient's part, but also on the therapist's--there have to be elements of risk, investment, trust, courage, self-disclosure, and so on. In Winnicottian terms, the true self must be evoked, which does not mean there cannot be all manner of false self defenses against interrelating and escapes into schizoid withdrawal. It does mean there must also be--in addition to the familiar avoidance of intimacy--a dawning recognition of the possibility of interpersonal contact that is worth exploring, entailing a minimal investment of the true self.

Unfortunately, the elaborate, artificial, hierarchical structure of the therapeutic situation makes it easy to lose sight of this, something that can be seen most clearly in what might be called false self therapy (which I discuss in great detail in my book, The Dark Side of the Analytic Moon, Alper, 1996) where there can be years of presumably ongoing treatment in which the real or true self relationship between patient and therapist has actually been deferred.

To sum up, the analysis of defenses and resistances is not therapeutic unless on some level there is also the participation of the true self. If the patient is therefore being defensive and resistive because essentially there is no need or psychic space created to involve the true self, then the therapy cannot be meaningful, regardless of how technically proficient. When defensiveness is in the service of the false self--and does not arise as a reaction to the presence of the true self--then what typically unfolds is one kind of power operation or another. And, sadly, all too often--because it is so painful it can feel deceptively real--this is taken by both patient and therapist for a genuine therapeutic encounter.

CONCLUSION

A power transaction has been defined as arising when there is a covert attempt to impose rules on the behavior of the other, rules that patently are meant to benefit only one person. Today the dynamics of such transactions are discussed from an increasingly politicized standpoint: typically in terms of the authoritarian abuses of people in power vis-á-vis the rights of the have nots, what I have called the civil rights of the self. By contrast, the phenomena of power that have been explored are primarily intrapsychic and interpersonal. In other words an attempt has been made to tease out--from the political, cultural and social institutionalization of power that to some extent must be implicated in individual power transactions--the personal as much as possible.

Although the dynamics and various patterns of behavior that are depicted are based on incidents reported and experienced by former patients of mine, they probably occur just as often to people who are not involved in therapy.

Some of these patterns are: the sociopathic use of power as exemplified in the code of the street, scams and con games versus the ordinary use of power typified by the everyday exercise of authoritarian roles; the dynamics of a power struggle and its relationship to the democratic way of life perhaps best illustrated by the classic American odd couple--boss-employee; the impact of the brush-off; the marketing of the self; the strategic relating of the salesman; the expression of unbridled contempt as a means of controlling the other; the psychology of the threat and of the good enforcer; the need for fair play as a defense against power operations; the difference between family-centered and adult intimacy; the unconscious desire of parents to bully their children; the tactics of humiliation; power plays such as beating someone to the punch, justifying any limit of outrageous behavior by referring to narcissistic honesty and the sanctimonious practice of tough love; the attempt to control the temperature of the relationship; the act of degrading someone; the dynamics of a street fight; the art of bluffing; being courageous as an object relation; the politics of relating; hierarchical nurturance; the politics of power; performing for love; pseudo autonomy; and therapy games as played by therapist and patient.

It is obvious, that the uses of power that have been delineated far more often than not have been abuses. This is no accident. A major theme of this book, as mentioned, is that intimacy, being an intrinsically complex state of mind difficult to achieve, occurs rarely in our present day culture. What is important is that it does exist and that therefore there is another style of relating that does not depend on a superiority of force and where the power one has lies muted in the background, ready to be in the service of the deeper needs of a true self seeking, not conquest of the other, but the conditions for intimate engagement.

REFERENCES

Alper, G. (1994). The Singles Scene. San Francisco: International Scholars Publications.

(1996). The Dark Side of the Analytic Moon.
Bethesda, Maryland: International Scholars Publications.

Adler, A. (1956). The Individual Psychology of Alfred Adler: A Systematic Presentation in Selections from his Writings, Edited by Heinz L. Ansbacher and Rowena R. Ansbacher. New York: Viking Press.

Berne, E. (1964). Games People Play. New York: Columbia University Press.

Bion, W. R. (1970). Attention and Interpretation. London: Tavistock Publications.

(1992). Cogitations. London: H. Karnac Books Ltd.

Bollas, C. (1987). The Shadow of the Object. New York: Columbia University Press.

(1993). Being a Character. New York: Hill and Wang, a division of Farrar, Straus and Giroux.

(1995). Preoccupation Unto Death and the Functions of History in Cracking Up. New York: Hill and Wang, a division of Farrar, Straus and Giroux.

Dawkins, R. (1996). Climbing Mt. Improbable. New York: W.W. Norton & Co.

Erikson, E. (1951). Childhood and Society. New York: W.W. Norton.

Freud, S. (1900). The Interpretation of Dreams. Standard Edition, 4&5. London: Hogarth Press, 1953.

(1923). The ego and the id. Standard Edition, 14:146-158. London: Hogarth Press, 1957.

Goffman, E. (1959). The Presentation of Self in Every Life. New York: Pantheon Book.

(1963). Stigma. New York: Simon and Schuster.

(1967). Interaction Ritual. New York: Pantheon.

Horgan, J. (1996). The End of Science. Reading, Massachusetts: Addison Wesley.

Jackson, D.D. and Haley, J. (1963). Therapy, communication and change. Vol. 1, Human Communication Series. Palo Alto, CA: Science and Behavior Books, 1968.

Khan, M.M.R. (1979). Alienation in Perversions. New York: International Universities Press.

Laing, R.D. and Esterson, A. (1964). Sanity, Madness and the Family. New York: Basic Books.

Laplanche, J. and Pontalis, B. (1973). The Language of Psychoanalysis. New York: W.W. Norton & Co.

Lorenz, K. On Aggression (1966). On Aggression. New York: Harcourt, Brace & World.

(1970). Studies in Animal and Human Behavior Vol. 1 Translated by Robert Martin. Cambridge, Massachusetts: Harvard University Press.

(1971). Studies in Animal and Human Behavior Vol. 2, Translated by Robert Martin. Cambridge, Massachusetts: Harvard University Press.

(1981). The Foundations of Ethology. New York: Simon and Schuster.

Phillips, A. (1996). Terrors and Experts. Cambridge, Massachusetts: Harvard University Press.

Racker, H. (1968). Transference and Counter-transference. New York: International Universities Press.

Sartre, J. (1956). Being and Nothingness. New York: Simon and Schuster.

(1957). Existentialism and Human Emotion. New York: Citadel Press Books.

Sullivan, H.S. (1953). The Interpersonal Theory of Psychiatry. New York: W.W. Norton & Co.

(1973). Clinical Studies in Psychiatry. New York: W.W. Norton.

Tinbergen, N. (1951). The Study of Instinct. London: Oxford University Press.

Winnicott, D.W. (1965). Ego distortion in terms of true and false self. In The maturational processes and the facilitating environment. New York: International Universities Press.

Wittgenstein, L. (1969). On certainty. New York: Harper and Row.

INDEX

110

112